ROYAL AIR FOR

No XV Squadron is unique in the RAF in maintaining the name of a World War 2 'Presentation aircraft' — a Short Stirling donated by the MacRobert family. On 1 April 1992 the name passed to Tornado GR1 ZA614 of the TWCU when No XV became that unit's 'shadow'. *Paul Jackson*

Ian Allan
abc

ROYAL AIR FORCE

Paul Jackson

IAN ALLAN
Publishing

Contents

Front cover:
British Aerospace/McDonnell Douglas Harrier GR7.

Rear cover, top:
An example of a station badge, Finningley's was granted in 1948. It is depicted with the crown of St Edward worn by HM Queen Elizabeth II. As Finningley straddles the Yorkshire/Nottinghamshire border, the badge combines the white rose and oak leaves of these counties. *Paul Jackson*

Rear cover, bottom:
Nos 2729 and 2890 Squadrons of the Royal Auxiliary Air Force are equipped with Oerlikon 35mm anti-aircraft guns captured from Argentina in 1982. *Paul Jackson*

First published 1992

ISBN 0 7110 2112 0

Published by Ian Allan Ltd, Shepperton, Surrey; and printed by Ian Allan Printing Ltd at their works at Coombelands in Runnymede, England.

Introduction

More by coincidence than design, this handbook appears as the Royal Air Force is in the midst of a significant reorganisation, the better to operate within the new strategic situation of the 1990s. RAF Germany has been halved in size, and one may expect that its remaining element will not have a long future once the last Russian aircraft have left the former East Germany in 1994. At home, the combat elements of Strike Command and the training and logistical units of Support Command are moving bases and, in some cases, disbanding. The defence budget is beginning to shrink, and now sitting alongside the Air Marshals in their light blue suits and brass hats are accountants and efficiency experts in pinstripe suits and bowler hats.

That said, it would be wrong to assume that the RAF is in decline. As a central pillar of NATO, the RAF shares in the credit for liberating the people of Eastern Europe without having fired a shot — surely, the best way to win a war, if only a cold one. For 40 years the communist wolf huffed and puffed from behind the Iron Curtain it had thrown across Europe, but when the NATO house failed to crumble the wolf collapsed from exhaustion. There is no honourable satisfaction to be gained from gloating over the present plight of the former USSR and its defunct empire. However, the current rationalisation under the government's 'Options for Change' programme is the RAF's justly-earned reward for helping to ensure that a similar fate did not befall us in the more prosperous West, as successive occupants of the Kremlin had long planned.

The unexpected collapse of Soviet imperialism between 1989 and 1991 was as cataclysmic as it was sudden and carried an important message to those responsible for determining the military strength of the United Kingdom: Cataclysmic events are usually unexpected and sudden. Whilst NATO is freed from the terrifying prospect of waking one morning to find Warsaw Pact tanks racing westward across the North German Plain, effective and vigilant military forces are still required. Whatever his faults, Saddam Hussein is owed a great debt by the West for a perfectly-timed reminder of that fact.

The RAF performed with great distinction in the Gulf War, but shortcomings were evident as a result of specialisation for a European conflict. These were patched-over with the initiative and versatility for which the RAF is justly renowned throughout the world, although that skill in making the best of a bad job will result in the important questions being brushed aside at political level with the diplomatic equivalent of, 'What's the fuss, we won, didn't we?'.

Another danger of the Gulf War concerns its 'one off' nature (*all* wars are one-offs), most clearly characterised by the abdication of the Iraqi Air Force. In view of air power's walk-over, the public is questioning the need for low-level flying practice instead of asking why, when it found it could operate with impunity at medium level, the RAF had no system on hand with which to capitalise on that advantage and was forced to put out an urgent call for the doughty Buccaneer and its laser-designators.

The challenge now facing the RAF and its political masters is one of adapting to changed situations — not merely pretending still to deter a phantom Warsaw Pact with a smaller air force. The next time the RAF is in combat — and most assuredly, there *will* be a next time — it may be fighting shoulder to shoulder with Poles, Czechs and even Russians; what it will not know until perhaps a few days before battle is the name of its adversary, the quality of his equipment, morale of the opposition and the terrain over which it will be in combat. If the next few years are used wisely, the RAF's comparatively small contraction will be seen as an opportunity to strengthen greatly its capabilities for a broader range of strategic possibilities. The White Paper, *Options for Change*, should have been titled 'Opportunity to Change for the Better'.

In this handbook will be found the current organisation and equipment of the RAF and explanations of its operational tasks and the role of the supporting services which, though remaining on the ground, are no less important than the more visible elements. The RAF completed a NATO-inspired build-up programme in 1990, reaching a peak which is unlikely to be seen again. Therefore, this 'snapshot' book is augmented by brief mention of disbandments since that time as both a historical record and an *aide memoire*.

Faced with the need to cover a broad spectrum of subjects, the author has sought not to compete with the overlapping, but far more detailed analyses of certain aspects to be found in companion volumes. *abc Military Aircraft Markings*, *abc Combat Aircraft Recognition*, *abc Air Traffic Control* and *abc Air Band Radio Guide* may therefore be regarded as subjects for further study. *Aficionados* of VHF/UHF radio monitoring and general air traffic procedures will find details in the last two books mentioned which — because they are common to both civil and military aviation — can find no place in this publication.

Tradition and technology. Both based at Coningsby, the Spitfire PRXIX of the Battle of Britain Memorial Flight and Tornado F3 of No 229 OCU are — in their own ways — equally potent symbols of today's Royal Air Force. *Geoff Lee/BAe*

Jaguar GR1A XZ364 returned from the 1991 Gulf War with this most appropriate nose-art. Could disciplining Third World bullies be a new role for the RAF now that the Warsaw Pact has evaporated? *Paul Jackson*

1 Stations

RAF aircraft currently operate from 35 bases which may be considered major flying stations and over 50 minor or joint-user aerodromes. The former are listed below with brief notes on their history and role; the latter appear in tabular form. Details given immediately following the name are the county (country for overseas bases); distance and direction from the nearest town; heading and length of the principal runway (with any secondary runway in parentheses) — see Chapter 7 for further details; and resident flying units. Where space permits, notable non-flying units are mentioned, but their inclusion is not intended to be comprehensive.

It will be noted that most major stations date from the expansion period of the RAF in the mid/late-1930s. They will be found to have a similar style of building, the most obvious feature of which is the concertina-roofed, Type C hangar, later examples of which lack the squared corners to the roof. In the early-war period, the domed-roof Type J hangar was introduced to simplify construction, examples being found at Coningsby and Lyneham, both dating from 1940. The few remaining stations opened in the mid-war years were built with corrugated-iron Type T2 (or similar) hangars

UK-style Phase 3 hardened aircraft shelters have sliding doors and a winch to pull aircraft back under cover (a process here being begun on a Tornado F3 of No 23 Squadron) *Paul Jackson*

which have been refurbished subsequently. Bases with a history of changed ownership reflect that in their architecture — a good example being Lossiemouth, which has adjacent Types C, J and T2 hangars on the main camp and Blister hangars and more Type Js across the airfield.

Aircraft enthusiasts are drawn to airfields to pursue their hobby from the outside. The data which follow make no attempt to identify vantage points at airfields. It must suffice to record that in a densely-populated island, most bases have roads from which landing — and even taxying — aircraft can be photographed. The RAF Police need to be vigilant in view of the terrorist threat, but co-operation and proof of identity, if questioned, are normally enough to satisfy the authorities. Damaging of crops to get closer to airfields surrounded by farmland reflects badly on all aviation enthusiasts and is to be deplored.

Collectors of serial numbers are advised below of those bases having hardened aircraft shelters (HAS) in which aircraft are kept when not flying. Other stations can be assumed to keep their aircraft on a flight-line during operating hours — those with large maritime and transport aircraft leaving them outdoors at all times other than when being overhauled.

Enthusiasts should clearly understand that the liberal attitude shown by the authorities towards their hobby in the UK is most definitely NOT shared throughout Europe — even in some EEC and NATO countries.

MAJOR UK BASES

Major Bases

● **ABINGDON** (Oxfordshire). Immediately west of Abingdon. 18/36 6,532ft (08/26 4,800ft). Closed 31 July 1992. Bulldog and Chipmunk aircraft transferred to Benson (qv). Re-location under way of the Engineering Wing including Nos 1, 2 and 3 Squadrons (overhaul of Jaguars, Hawks and Buccaneers, respectively, all transferred to St Athan); RAF Exhibition Flight, mainly with cockpit sections and full-size plastic replica aircraft; Battle Damage Repair School with training airframes; and Repair & Salvage Squadron, transporting damaged aircraft.

● **AKROTIRI** (Cyprus). Southwest of Limassol in British Sovereign Base Area — inaccessible to enthusiasts. 10/28 8,993ft. No 84 Squadron, Wessex HC5C. Built 1956 as a strategic base and now major staging post, which was heavily used in connection with 1991 Gulf War. Armament Practice Camp (APC) for Tornado F3s, which are resident for three-week rotations, assisted by banner-towing Hawks of No 100 Squadron from Wyton. Wessex provide SAR cover for APC, transport for visiting army detachments and security patrols and occasional support for United Nations. In east of Cyprus, RAF Kingsfield is rudimentary emergency airfield.

● **BELIZE CITY** (Belize). International airport of Belize (formerly British Honduras) in Central America. No 1417 Flight (four Harrier GR3s); No 1563 Flight (four Puma HC1s). RAF detachment present since 1975 to counter threat from Guatemala, which claims some territory in Belize. Aircraft and personnel rotated from units in Europe, Harrier GR3 being due for possible replacement by GR5. RAF Regiment has Rapier SAM detachment.

● **BENSON** (Oxfordshire). Two miles northeast of Wallingford. 01/19 5,981ft. The Queen's Flight (BAe 146 CC2 and Wessex HCC4); No 115 Squadron (Andover E3/E3A, London UAS and Oxford UAS, Bulldog T1); No 6 AEF (Chipmunk T10); No 612 VGS (Vigilant T1); detachment No 241 OCU from Brize Norton (BAe 146 CC2); and Andover Training Flight (Andover E3/E3A). Opened 1939 and became famous as a photo-reconnaissance base; home of royal flying since May 1946. Wessex Maintenance Unit overhauls and re-paints Wessex of No 72 Squadron. Benson received its two UASs and the AEF from Abingdon in July 1992 and will be home to a new squadron of Wessex HC2s and Pumas — possibly No 66.

● **BRAWDY** (Dyfed). Eight miles northwest of Haverfordwest. 02/20 7,369ft (15/33 (6,006ft). 'B' Flight of No 202 Squadron (Sea King HAR3). Opened as an RAF station in 1944, but transferred to the Fleet Air Arm two years later. Regained by the RAF in 1974, the base was used for weapons training, initially with Hunters, but from 1977 by Hawks of No 1 TWU (Nos 79 and 234 Squadrons). The TWU closed on 31 August 1992.

● **BRIZE NORTON** (Oxfordshire). Five miles southeast of Burford. 08/26 10,007ft. Military Emergency Diversion Airfield (see Chapter 7). No 10 Squadron (VC10 C1); No 101 Squadron (VC10 K2/K3); No 216 Squadron (TriStar K1/KC1/C2); and No 241 OCU (TriStar and VC10). Opened 1937 and used by the Airborne Forces during World War 2. Major extensions by the USAF between

1950 and 1965, when it reverted to the RAF as a transport base. Joint Air Transport Establishment, in two Type D hangars on the southeast side, and related Air Movements School have a few training airframes. No 1 Parachute Training School uses Lyneham's Hercules for drops over Weston-on-the-Green, and elsewhere. The Air Loadmaster School is another resident. Brize is the RAF's main strategic transport base with regular TriStar and VC10 C1 services around the globe. Hemp-coloured VC10 K2/K3s are the main aerial tanker force and are shortly to be augmented by five VC10 K4s and tanker conversions of eight C1s. No 241 OCU aircraft are borrowed from the squadrons, as required, the unit's BAe 146 detachment being at Benson. Major servicing of VC10s in the large Base Hangar will transfer to St Athan.

● **BRUGGEN** (Germany). West of Monchengladbach, adjacent to the Dutch border. 09/27 8,159ft. Nos IX, 14, 17 and 31 Squadrons (Tornado GR1). Selected as the sole RAF strike/attack base in Germany following the disbandment of Laarbruch-based squadrons. With Geilenkirchen, Laarbruch and Wildenrath, the base was built during the early-1950s to secure air assets from a rapid Warsaw pact advance by placing them as far west as possible. Opened in May 1953, it has always been associated with strike/attack roles, the Tornado having replaced Jaguars in 1984-85. Also resident, No 431 MU is unusual for a Maintenance Unit in the diversity of its roles. In addition to modifying and repairing aircraft, it stores equipment as far removed as avionics and furniture for married quarters. Aircraft are operated from HAS sites and are difficult to observe from outside the base.

● **CHIVENOR** (Devon). Immediately southeast of Braunton. 10/28 6,012ft. No 7 FTS (Nos 19 and 92 Squadrons), Hawk T1A/T1 (known as No 2 TWU until mid-1992); 'A' Flight of No 22 Squadron, Wessex HC2; and No 624 VGS, Vigilant T1. Originally a civilian aerodrome, Chivenor was taken-over by the RAF in World War 2 and used by Coastal Command, but since the end of the conflict has been a fighter training base. A long association with the Hunter ended when the base closed for fixed-wing operations in 1974, but after extensive rebuilding of the camp, Chivenor re-opened in 1980 to accommodate Hawks. The Wessex detachment is kept busy during the summer months, being responsible for a popular holiday coastline.

● **CHURCH FENTON** (West Yorkshire). Five miles SSE of Tadcaster. 06/24 5,774ft (16/34 5,466ft). No 7 FTS (Tucano T1). Closure of Church Fenton as a principal station was planned before the end of 1992, but the airfield will be retained as a relief landing ground after much of the camp and surrounding land has been sold. A fighter base when opened in 1937, Church Fenton turned to support duties in 1959. After four years of temporary closure, it re-opened in 1979 with Jet Provost T3A/T5As until converted to Tucanos, the first student flying beginning in December 1989. A few Jet Provost T5As were retained in 1990-91 for use by the Refresher Flying Flight. Elvington was employed as a relief landing ground, but will be disposed of in 1993. No 7 FTS Tucanos are being transferred to No 1 FTS at Linton-on-Ouse and elsewhere.

● **COLTISHALL** (Norfolk). Eight miles NNE of Norwich. 04/22 7,500ft. Nos 6, 41 and 54 Squadrons (Jaguar GR1A/T2A); and 'E' Flight of No 22 Squadron (Wessex HC2). Assigned to attack and reconnaissance roles, Jaguars of the Coltishall Wing distinguished themselves in the Gulf War of 1991 and were later based in Turkey to watch over Iraqi Kurdistan. The base opened as a fighter station in 1940 and remained thus until Jaguars began arriving in 1974. Squadrons are expected to keep their equipment until it is replaced by the Eurofighter EFA at the end of the 1990s, but the units may move to a Suffolk base to acquire HAS accommodation. Jaguars currently operate from a flight-line as their wartime role is to re-deploy as reinforcements for the NATO flanks.

● **CONINGSBY** (Lincolnshire). Eight miles SSW of Horncastle. 08/26 9,000ft. Nos 5 and 29 Squadrons, No 229 OCU (No 65 Reserve Squadron) and F3OEU (Tornado F3); and Battle of Britain Memorial Flight (Lancaster BI, Hurricane IIC, Spitfire IIA, VB, PR XIX, Devon C2/2 and Chipmunk T10). The first of three Tornado interceptor bases, Coningsby housed bombers from 1940 until the first Phantoms arrived in 1968. Tornado deliveries began in 1984 and the last Phantom (on completion of a local overhaul) left the base on 16 October 1987. No 229 OCU provides Tornado F3 pilots and navigators and the F3 Operational Evaluation Unit is

Stations of RAF Germany were first to have the HAS and most are Phase 1 buildings with angular sides and a 'porch' for the hinged doors. Tornado GR1 of No 17 Squadron at Brüggen. *Paul Jackson*

Church Fenton was built for fighters, so its Type C hangars have only nine bays, instead of the full 13. Tucano of No 7 FTS. *Paul Jackson*

responsible to HQ Strike Command for developing operational procedures and evaluating new equipment. The two squadrons operate from HAS sites, but the other aircraft use the flight-line. The BoBMF hangars are open to visitors on *most* weekdays (Tel: 0526 44041).

● **COTTESMORE** (Leicestershire). Five miles northeast of Oakham. 05/23 9,003ft. Trinational Tornado Training Establishment (Tornado GR1/IDS). All conversion training for the interdictor/strike version of Tornado is undertaken at Cottesmore, where the TTTE received its first aircraft in 1980. The unit trains German and Italian students alongside those of the RAF, but crews are posted to other bases (Honington in the case of the RAF) to learn combat procedures. Tornados from Germany and Italy are included in the Cottesmore fleet, and the base naturally attracts visiting transport aircraft from those countries. Flying is conducted by the Tornado OCU, comprising 'A', 'B', 'C' and 'S' (Standards) Squadrons, although badges on the aircraft are representative only. The base opened in 1938 and housed both Victor and Vulcan V-bombers during the 1950s and 1960s. A large parking ramp was constructed for Tornado operations.

● **CRANWELL** (Lincolnshire). Four miles northwest of Sleaford. 09/27 6,293ft (01/19 4,803ft). No 3 FTS (Tucano T1). This former Royal Naval Air Service airship station, opened in 1915, is famous as the home of the RAF College, its flying component being No 3 FTS. The school's last Jet Provost left on 29 October 1991, Tucano deliveries having begun in December 1990. Barkston Heath is the principal satellite, but Cranwell North is a grass airfield across the (B1429) road from the main site. Interesting architecture includes a variety of hangars and other buildings spanning over half a century. All future RAF officers pass through Cranwell for at least (since 1979) their 18-week Initial Officer Training Course, those from University Air Squadron proceeding to No 3 FTS for flying training. Other elements include the Headquarters University Air Squadrons and Department of Air Warfare. Engineering trainees of the Department of Special Ground Training have a fleet of grounded Hunters in a hangar on the southeast corner of the airfield.

● **FINNINGLEY** (West Yorkshire). Five miles southeast of Doncaster. 02/20 8,993ft. No 6 FTS (Dominie T1, Jet Provost T5/T5A and Jetstream T1); Yorkshire UAS (Bulldog T1); No 9 AEF (Chipmunk T10); and (until 1 October 1992) HQ UK SAR Wing (Wessex HC2 and Sea King HAR3). Finningley's main role is training of most non-pilot aircrew (navigators, air electronics and air engineer personnel) on Dominies and Jet Provosts. The JPs, which will be replaced by a combination of Tucanos and Hawks, are operated by the Low Level & Air Defence Squadron. Jetstreams equip the Multi-Engine Training Squadron, which converts students from single-engined aircraft and prepares them for flying large transports and maritime aircraft. The civilian airfield at Gamston is used as a satellite by Bulldogs. HQ UK SAR Wing comprised HQ Flights of Nos 22 and 202 Squadrons; Engineering Squadron (Wessex and Sea King overhauls, including Sea Kings of No 78 Squadron from the Falkland Islands); SARTU at Valley; and SKTF at Culdrose. HQ 22 and helicopter engineering support moved to St Mawgan on 1 October 1992, when HQ 202 relocated to Boulmer. Opened in 1936, Finningley was mainly a bomber and bomber-training base until the present residents began arriving from 1970 onwards.

● **GUTERSLOH** (Germany). Three miles west of Gütersloh. 09/27 7,388ft. Nos 3 and 4 Squadrons (Harrier GR7); and No 18 Squadron (Chinook HC1B and Puma HC1). Sole major RAF base east of the Rhine, Gütersloh is programmed for closure on 1 April 1993. Built in 1935 for the Luftwaffe and taken over by the RAF 10 years later, the base retains its German style of buildings, despite HAS sites for the two Harrier squadrons and a new, large hangar to accommodate Chinooks. Nearby army bases generate transport aircraft movements, including civilian passenger charters. All four resident squadrons are equipped to take to the field in the event of war and operate from dispersed sites in support of the army. Harriers will move to Laarbruch, as will some of the helicopters: Nos 3 and 4 in October/November 1992 and No 18 in March 1993.

● **HONINGTON** (Suffolk). Seven miles NNE of Bury St Edmunds. 09/27 9,012ft. No 13 Squadron (Tornado GR1A); Tornado Weapons Conversion Unit (No XV Reserve Squadron) (Tornado GR1). Despite extensive facilities, including two HAS sites, Honington is to lose its current residents, but may be retained for other purposes. It has been operational since 1937. The TWCU provides operational training to pilots and navigators who have qualified on the Tornado at Cottesmore before they join a squadron. It will move to Lossiemouth in mid-1993. At the same time, the reconnaissance-tasked No 13 Squadron will transfer to Marham, together with the Groundcrew Reconnaissance Training Facility and Tornado Electronic Warfare Maintenance School. On 1 April 1992, TWCU adopted the reserve ('shadow') identity of No XV Squadron, having formerly been No 45 (Reserve) Squadron. It normally operates from the flight-line, No 13 squadron being in the northwestern HAS complex.

● **KINLOSS** (Grampian). Three miles northeast of Forres. 08/26 7,582ft. Nos 120, 201 and 206 Squadrons (Nimrod MR2); and, No 662 VGS (Viking T1). For a long period the RAF's principal maritime reconnaissance base, the station became the sole Nimrod MR2 operator in 1992, receiving No 236 OCU from St Mawgan in the latter part of that year. However, St Mawgan will be retained as a forward operating base. Of 33 Nimrods available, the force will be reduced to 26 operational and the remainder in storage or as in-use spares. Aircraft do not carry individual squadron insignia. Kinloss has developed strong maritime reconnaissance traditions since it opened in 1939. Across the airfield from the main camp, the Nimrod Major Servicing Unit (formed 1 February 1972) is responsible for overhauls, including the R1s of No 51 Squadron.

● **LAARBRUCH** (Germany). Three miles southwest of Weeze. 10/28 8,012ft. The last of the 'Clutch' bases (Brüggen, Geilenkirchen, Laarbruch and Wildenrath) built with German war reparations, Laarbruch opened in October 1954 and has been involved with strike/attack aircraft ever since. It is now in a period of change, following the running-down of its Tornado GR1 force: No 16 Squadron disbanded in September 1991, followed by No XV on 31 March 1992 and No 20 on 31 July, whilst the reconnaissance-tasked No II moved to RAF Marham in December 1991. Expected in replacement are Nos 3 and 4 Squadrons with Harrier GR7s from Gütersloh and a combined helicopter squadron with some Chinooks of No 18 Squadron and

Pumas of No 230 Squadron, also from Gütersloh.

● **LEEMING** (North Yorkshire). Six miles southwest of Northallerton. 16/34 7,520ft. Nos 11, 23 and 25 Squadrons (Tornado F3); Northumbrian UAS (Bulldog T1); and, No 11 AEF (Chipmunk T10). Dating from 1940, this former bomber and training station was extensively rebuilt in the late-1980s in preparation for the Tornado. No 11 Squadron operates from the original hangars, but the other two units are in HAS sites. The first squadron, No 11, formed here in July 1988 and the last, No 25, was declared operational in January 1990.

● **LEUCHARS** (Fife). Four miles northwest of St Andrews. 09/27 8,491ft (04/22 4,803ft). Military Emergency Diversion Airfield (see Chapter 7). Nos 43 and 111 Squadrons (Tornado F3); 'B' Flight of No 22 Squadron (Wessex HC2); Aberdeen, Dundee and St Andrews UAS (Bulldog T1). The third and last permanent Tornado F3 base re-equipped its resident squadrons during 1989-90 and the era of the Phantom ended in January 1991 when No 228 OCU disbanded, the final aircraft leaving in April. Leuchars is the oldest of Scotland's military airfields, having begun as a balloon station in 1911. A long-standing maritime connection ended with the installation of fighters in 1950.

● **LINTON-ON-OUSE** (North Yorkshire). Eight miles northwest of York. 04/22 6,020ft (10/28 4,394ft). No 1 FTS (Jet Provost T3A/T5A); Royal Navy Elementary FTS (Bulldog T1); and No 642 VGS (Vigilant T1). Final operator of the Jet Provost, No 1 FTS is converting to Tucano T1s, including aircraft transferred from No 7 FTS at Church Fenton in 1992. The RNEFTS is detached to Topcliffe for 60 hours' flying training of naval students before they convert to helicopters or Sea Harriers at the RN's own training units. On 7 July 1993 the RNEFTS is to be taken-over by a civilian contractor, probably using a different type of aircraft. Dishforth is used as a relief landing ground. Linton's background is as a bomber base from 1937 and a fighter station postwar, until the arrival of No 1 FTS in 1957.

● **LOSSIEMOUTH** (Grampian). Four miles north of Elgin. 05/23 9,091ft (10/28 6,025ft). Nos 12 and 208 Squadrons (Buccaneer S2B, Hunter T7/T7A/T8B); No 226

Above:
The new air traffic control tower at Leeming is nicknamed the 'Happy Eater' because the associated buildings are of a similar style to a motorway service-area. Pictured in the foreground is a Tornado F3 of No 11 Squadron. *Paul Jackson*

Below:
Three Shackleton AEW2s (now withdrawn) overfly an interesting hangar selection at Lossiemouth. Type T2 (centre left), Type J (upper right) and full size Type C (lower right). More Type Js and Blister hangars are on the opposite side of the airfield. *Paul Jackson*

OCU (Jaguar GR1A/T2A); and 'D' Flight of No 202 Squadron (Sea King HAR3). Opened in 1939, 'Lossie' was an RAF training base in World War 2, then became a Fleet Air Arm shore station until 1972. The Buccaneer force operates from hardened shelters in the maritime strike/attack role, although the associated No 237 OCU disbanded in October 1991. A further withdrawal, in June 1991 concerned the Shackleton AEW2s of No 8 Squadron, which now flies Sentries at Waddington. Despite these reductions, Lossiemouth is a busy base with numerous short-term training detachments and it is expected that activities will increase in future. No 226 OCU, responsible for Jaguar pilot training, adopted the reserve identity of No 16 Squadron in November 1991. To replace Buccaneers, two Marham Tornado GR1 squadrons will arrive in 1993 and convert to carrying Sea Eagle anti-ship missiles before the end of 1994. No 617 Squadron will retain its identity following the transfer in October 1993, but No 27 will arrive at Lossiemouth in April of that year and become No 12 when that Buccaneer unit disbands.

● **LYNEHAM** (Wiltshire). Ten miles southwest of Swindon. 18/36 5,991ft. Nos 24,30, 47 and 70 Squadrons and No 242 OCU (Hercules C1/C1(K)/C3). Home of the entire RAF Hercules force apart from two C1(K) tankers based in the Falkland Islands on rotation, Lyneham opened in 1940 and has been a transport base for all but the first two years of its existence. It sees a variety of foreign visitors. Hercules are operated in a central pool and carry no unit markings. Also resident is the UK Mobile Air Movements Squadron which is responsible for establishing handling facilities at any temporary base adopted as an airhead.

● **MARHAM** (Norfolk). Seven miles southeast of King's Lynn. 06/24 9,140ft (01/19 5,900ft). Nos II, 27 and 617 Squadrons (Tornado GR1/GR1A); and No 55 Squadron (Victor K2). Marham opened in 1937 and has maintained a long association with bomber aircraft, although the last survivors of Britain's V-bombers are used in the tanking role and will be withdrawn when No 55 Squadron disbands in October 1993. No 2 Squadron arrived from Germany with reconnaissance-configured Tornado GR1As in December 1991, joining the longer-term strike/attack squadrons, Nos 27 and 617, which are based in two HAS sites. No 27

moves to Lossiemouth in April 1993 and will be replaced by No 13 Squadron from Honington two months later. No 617 goes to Lossiemouth in October 1993.

● **MOUNT PLEASANT** (Falkland Islands). 28 miles WSW of Port Stanley. 10/28 8,500ft (05/23 5,000ft). No 78 Squadron (Sea King HAR3 and Chinook HC1B); No 1312 Flight (Hercules C1(K)); and No 1435 Flight (Phantom FGR2 [Tornado F3 planned]). The RAF's newest aerodrome was officially opened on 12 May 1985 to deter Argentina from a further attempt to invade the Falkland Islands. The base has a minimal establishment of four fighters, two Hercules, two Chinooks and two Sea Kings, but has considerable accommodation and armament stocks for reinforcement attack, interceptor and maritime reconnaissance aircraft flown directly from the UK with tanker support. Tornado F3s were expected to replace the Phantoms in July 1992.

Mount Pleasant

FALKLAND ISLANDS

● **NORTHOLT** (Greater London). Three miles ENE of Uxbridge. 07/25 5,525ft. No 32 Squadron (Andover C1/C1(PR)/CC2, BAe 125 C1/C2/C3, Islander CC2 and Gazelle HT3). London's military airport was built as a fighter base in 1915 and retained defensive commitments until the end of World War 2, when its present role was adopted. Operations are restricted by the proximity of Heathrow, at which large visiting aircraft must land because of Northolt's comparatively short runway. Nevertheless, the base handles a multitude of foreign military transport and communications aircraft. Its complement was increased early in 1992 with the addition of Andovers from the disbanded No 60 Squadron at Wildenrath.

● **ODIHAM** (Hampshire). Seven miles east of Basingstoke. 10/28 6,027ft. No 7 Squadron (Chinook HC1B); No 33 Squadron (Puma HC1); and, No 240 OCU (Chinook HC1B and Puma HC1). Odiham is the home of the RAF Support Helicopter Force, which is dedicated to airlifting the army and its equipment at home and overseas. Opened in 1937, it has been a helicopter base since 1960, although the runway is kept operational for occasional fixed-wing visitors.

● **ST ATHAN** (South Glamorgan). 12 miles southwest of Cardiff. 08/26 5,988ft. University of Wales Air Squadron (Bulldog T1); and No 634 VGS (Viking T1). Despite its minor flying units, St Athan qualifies as a major base by reason of the maintenance activities of its Aircraft Engineering Wing located on the north, west and south of the airfield. St Athan supports most front-line aircraft and undertakes modification programmes and major overhauls. In 1991-92 it absorbed the Hawk, Jaguar and Buccaneer work formerly undertaken at Abingdon and VC10 overhauls from Brize Norton. No 4 School of Technical Training, on the eastern side, includes instructional airframes.

● **ST MAWGAN** (Cornwall). Four miles northeast of Newquay. 13/31 8,984ft. Military Emergency Diversion Airfield (see Chapter 7). No 42 Squadron and No 236 OCU (No 38 Reserve Squadron) (Nimrod MR2). St Mawgan will have no permanently-based units after No 42 Squadron disbands in August 1992 and No 236 OCU moves up to Kinloss soon afterwards. The base was opened in 1943 and later extensively rebuilt, resulting in a non-standard layout for an RAF station. After departure of the Nimrods, it will remain an important forward operating base for defence of the South-Western Approaches, housing periodic detachments of Nimrods and Buccaneers (the latter in HAS accommodation, and later to be replaced by Tornados). In mid-1992 it accepted non-flying units prior to the closure of Mount Batten, these being the School of Combat Survival & Rescue and No 3 Maritime Headquarters. HQ No 22 Squadron (Wessex) arrived from Finningley on 1 October 1992, to be followed by the Sea King Training Unit from RNAS Culdrose on 1 April 1993.

● **SCAMPTON** (Lincolnshire). Five miles north of Lincoln. 05/23 8,990ft. Central Flying School (Jet Provost T3A/T5A, Bulldog T1, Tucano T1 and Hawk T1A). Scampton was a bomber base from 1936 until 1982, before receiving the CFS HQ in 1984. The unit trains instructors and is disbanding its

JP squadron and increasing the Tucano complement. Resident Hawks are flown by the 'Red Arrows' aerobatic team. For convenience of servicing and operational considerations, CFS maintains major detachments at other bases: Hawk T1s with the similarly-equipped No 4 FTS at Valley; Gazelle HT3s at Shawbury; and various sailplanes at Syerston. Chipmunks are borrowed, as required. The Trade Management Training School has four Hunter F6s and two Hunter T7s in taxyable condition.

● **VALLEY** (Gwynedd). Five miles southeast of Holyhead. 14/32 7,520ft (01/19 5,381ft). No 4 FTS (Hawk T1); 'C' Flight of No 22 Squadron and SAR Training Unit (Wessex HC2). Valley began as a fighter base in 1941 and changed to training 10 years later. This remains its role, the FTS providing a 100-hour Hawk course, including weapons training, after the Tucano or Jet Provost phase. Nearby Mona is used as a relief landing ground. SARTU (formed 1979) trains all rescue helicopter aircrew for at least their basic stage, future Sea King personnel then going to the SKTU at Culdrose (St Mawgan from April 1993). Valley is the base for aircraft firing missiles at annual camps with the Strike Command Air-to-Air Missile Establishment. (Jindivik, Chukar and Stiletto unmanned targets are provided by DRA Llanbedr.)

● **WADDINGTON** (Lincolnshire). Four miles south of Lincoln. 03/21 9,000ft. No 8 Squadron and Sentry Training Squadron (Sentry AEW1); and, Vulcan Display Flight (Vulcan B2). Re-constructed in 1937, Waddington's long history as a bomber base ended in 1984, when an immediate change to Nimrod AEW3s was envisaged. Because of insurmountable problems with the aircraft's radar, it was not until July 1991 that No 8 Squadron re-formed at Waddington in the AEW role — with Sentries. Foreign fighter aircraft using the privately-operated (BAe) air combat manoeuvring range over the North Sea usually fly from Waddington, and the base is well utilised by overseas visitors to national air defence exercises and by training aircraft from Scampton and elsewhere. The VDF is parented by No 55 Squadron at Marham and has one airworthy Vulcan.

● **WATTISHAM** (Suffolk). Ten miles northwest of Ipswich. 05/23 7,490ft. Nos 56 and 74 Squadrons (Phantom FGR2). The future of Wattisham is uncertain following the run-down of its interceptor squadrons. No 56 was 'de-declared' from NATO on 30 June 1992, followed by No 74 on 31 September 1992. In January 1991, No 74 converted from the unique F-4J(UK) Phantom and gained a few extra aircraft for use by the Phantom Training Flight, although this disbanded at the end of the same year. The squadrons had a commitment to provide some crews for No 1435 Flight in the Falkland Islands until July 1992. Phantoms from Leuchars and Wildenrath have returned to Wattisham for salvage and scrapping. Opened in 1939, the base will close as an active RAF station in mid-1993 but may be returned as a forward operating base for air defence aircraft or assigned to other military roles.

● **WITTERING** (Cambridgeshire). Three miles south of Stamford. 08/26 9,050ft. No 1 Squadron and No 233 OCU (No 20 Reserve Squadron) (Harrier GR5/GR3/T4/T4A). With its rear entrance in Leicestershire, this unusually large RAF station (incorporating the former Collyweston airfield) ironically operates STO/VL fighter-bombers. However, there is ample space within the boundary for several training sites on which the Harrier can practice dispersed operations. Opened in 1916, the base has a varied selection of aircraft accommodation, including only one Type C hangar. It became the world's first STO/VL combat aircraft base in 1969. Mk 3 and 4 Harriers are flown alongside Mk 5s by the OCU, which

adopted the dual identity of No 20 (Reserve) Squadron in September 1992. No 1 Squadron will convert to GR7s and the OCU's GR3s will be withdrawn after the similarly-equipped No 1417 Flight in Belize is converted or disbanded.

● **WYTON** (Cambridgeshire). Three miles northeast of Huntingdon. 09/27 8,255ft. No 51 Squadron (Nimrod R1); No 100 Squadron (Hawk T1/T1A); No 360 Squadron (Canberra T17/T17A/E15); Canberra Training Flight (Canberra T4); and No 1 PRU (Canberra PR9). Unusual roles predominate at this station, No 51 Squadron's three Nimrods undertaking electronic reconnaissance, while No 100 is a target facilities unit and No 360 jams air and surface radars to give operators experience of working an a high ECM environment. No 1 PRU (formed 1 May 1982) is assigned to mapping and survey duties. Resident Electronic Warfare Operational Support Establishment includes the EW Avionic Unit (formed 1 June 1976) which is responsible for special installations, but now has to permanent allocation of aircraft. Also here is the Joint School of Photo Interpretation. The base opened in 1939.

Intended for V-bombers, but now containing Harrier GR5s, is the Gaydon-type hangar at Wittering. Note the cut-out for high tail fins. *Paul Jackson*

MINOR AERODROMES AND RANGES

18

Minor Aerodromes

RAF flying activities of a minor nature are undertaken at the aerodromes listed below. In the case of the Defence Research Agency (Aerospace Division) — known until 1991 as the Royal Aerospace Establishment — these are MoD airfields at which RAF and other aircraft are used for trials. The installations themselves are not necessarily small, as some units are lodged at civil airports. Only main runway details are given and installations which are not wholly RAF or at which it is a lodger are indicated by an asterisk.

● Aberporth*	Dyfed	08/26 3,002ft	DRA
● Aldergrove*	Ulster	07/25 9,111ft	No 72 Squadron (Wessex HC2)
● Arbroath*	Tayside	08/26 3,900ft	No 662 VGS (Viking T1)
● Barkston Heath	Lincs	06/24 6,000ft	Satellite for Cranwell
● Bedford*	Beds	09/27 10,500ft	DRA
● Binbrook	Lincs	03/21 7,498ft	No 643 VGS (Vigilant T1)
● Boscombe Down*	Wilts	06/24 10,537ft	Strike/Attack Operational Evaluation Unit (Harrier GR7, Tornado GR1 and Jaguar T2A), A&AEE and ETPS
● Boulmer	N'Humbs	Nil	A/202 Sqdn (Sea King HAR3)
● Bournemouth*	Dorset	08/26 6,030ft	No 2 AEF (Chipmunk T10)
● Cambridge*	Cambs	05/23 6,447ft	Cambridge UAS (Bulldog T1) and No 5 AEF (Chipmunk T10)
● Catterick	N Yorks	Grass	No 645 VGS (Viking T1)
● Chetwynd	Salop	Grass	RLG for Shawbury
● Cosford	Salop	06/24 3,770ft	Birmingham UAS (Bulldog T1) and No 633 VGS (Vigilant T1)
● Culdrose*	Cornwall	Helicopter only	SKTF (Sea King HAR3)
● Decimomannu*	Sardinia	17/35 9,810ft	RAF Support Unit
● Dishforth*	N Yorks	16/34 6,096ft	RLG for Linton-on-Ouse
● Edinburgh*	Lothian	07/25 8,400ft	E Lowlands UAS (Bulldog T1) and No 12 AEF (Chipmunk T10)
● Elvington	N Yorks	08/26 5,290ft	RLG for Church Fenton (Closed late-1992)
● Exeter*	Devon	08/26 6,834ft	No 4 AEF (Chipmunk T10)
● Farnborough*	Hants	07/25 7,874ft	Institute of Aviation Medicine (Hunter T7 and Jaguar T2A) and Defence Research Agency
● Filton*	Avon	10/28 8,038ft	Bristol UAS (Bulldog T1)
● Gatow	Germany	08/26 6,014ft	Station Flight (Chipmunk T10)
● Glasgow*	S'clyde	05/23 8,720ft	Glasgow & Strathclyde UAS (Bulldog T1)
● Goose Bay	Canada	08/26 11,050ft	Tornado detachment
● Halton	Bucks	Grass	No 613 VGS (Vigilant T1)
● Henlow	Beds	Grass	No 616 VGS (Vigilant T1)
● Hullavington	Glos	05/23 4,000ft	No 3 AEF (Chipmunk T10)
● Kenley	Kent	Grass	No 615 VGS (Viking T1)
● Kirknewton*	Lothian	Grass	No 661 VGS (Viking T1)
● Leconfield*	Humber	Helicopters	E/202 Sqn (Sea King HAR3)
● Lee-on-Solent*	Hants	05/23 4,348ft	Southampton UAS (Bulldog T1)
● Lt Rissington*	Glos	05/23 4,900ft	No 637 VGS (Vigilant T1)
● Llanbedr*	Gwynedd	18/36 7,500ft	DRA
● Macrihanish	S'clyde	11/29 10,003ft	Reserve maritime base
● Manston*	Kent	11/29 9,029ft	C/202 Sqn (Sea King HAR3), No 1 AEF (Chipmunk T10) and No 617 VGS (Viking T1)
● Mona	Gwynedd	04/22 5,466ft	RLG for Valley
● Newton	Notts	Grass	E Midlands UAS (Bulldog T1) and No 7 AEF (Chipmunk T10)
● North Front	Gibraltar	09/27 6,000ft	Temporary detachments
● Predannack*	Cornwall	05/23 5,950ft	No 626 VGS (Viking T1)

● Samlesbury*	Lancs	07/25 4,934ft	No 635 VGS (Vigilant T1)
● Sealand	Cheshire	Grass	No 631 VGS (Viking T1)
● Sek Kong*	Hong Kong	Helicopters	No 28 Squadron (Wessex HC2)
● Shawbury	Salop	01/19 6,018ft	No 2 FTS (Gazelle HT3 and Wessex HC2) and No 8 AEF (Chipmunk T10)
● South Cerney	Glos	Grass	No 625 VGS (Viking T1)
● Swansea*	W Glam	04/22 4,829ft	No 636 VGS (Viking T1)
● Swanton Morley	Norfolk	Grass	No 611 VGS (Viking T1)
● Swinderby	Lincs	06/24 6,088ft	Elementary FTS (Chipmunk T10)
● Sydenham*	Ulster	04/22 6,001ft	Queen's UAS (Bulldog T1) and No 13 AEF (Bulldog T1)
● Syerston	Notts	07/25 5,900ft	Air Cadets' Central Gliding School (Vigilant T1, Valiant T1, Viking T1 and Janus C) and No 644 VGS (Vigilant T1)
● Stornoway*	Hebrides	18/36 7,612ft	Reserve interceptor base
● Ternhill*	Salop	05/23 3,215ft	No 632 VGS (Vigilant T1)
● Topcliffe*	N Yorks	03/21 6,027ft	RLG for Linton-on-Ouse
● Upavon	Wilts	Grass	No 622 VGS (Viking T1)
● West Freugh*	Dumfries	06/24 5,997f	DRA
● West Malling*	Kent	07/25 6,000ft	No 618 VGS (Viking T1)
● Weston-s-Mare*	Avon	07/25 4,200ft	No 621 VGS (Viking T1)
● West Raynham	Norfolk	03/21 6,000ft	Occasional use only
● Wethersfield*	Essex	10/28 9,088ft	No 614 VGS (Viking T1)
● Wideawake	Ascension		Staging post to Falklands
● Wildenrath	Germany	09/27 8,192ft	Closed April 1992
● Woodvale	Mersey	04/22 4,754ft	Liverpool UAS & Manchester UAS (Bulldog T1) and No 10 AEF (Chipmunk T10)

NOTES:

RLG: Relief Landing Ground. Usually parented by a training unit to reduce circuit congestion at the main base.

A&AEE: Aircraft and Armament Evaluation Establishment. Operated by MoD (Procurement Executive). Fleet includes some RAF aircraft.

ETPS: Empire Test Pilots' School. As A&AEE.

Wildenrath: Former residents were No 19 Squadron (Phantom FGR2) disbanded January 1992; No 60 Squadron (Andover C1/C1(PR)/CC2) disbanded 31 March 1992; and, No 92 Squadron (Phantom FGR2) disbanded July 1991.

Weapons Ranges

● Cape Wrath	Highland
● Cowden	Humberside
● Donna Nook	Lincolnshire
● Garvie Island	Highland (1)
● Holbeach	Lincolnshire
● Jurby	Isle of Man
● Nordhorn	Germany
● Otterburn	Northumberland (2)
● Pembrey	Dyfed
● Rosehearty	Aberdeenshire
● Spadeadam	Cumbria (2)
● South Uist	Hebrides (3)
● Tain	Ross-shire
● Wainfleet	Lincolnshire

(1) Used for live bombing
(2) Time-expired aircraft used as targets
(3) RAF and Army Rapier SAM firing

2 Flying units

Today's RAF has some 60 squadrons, supported by a larger number of units providing them with aircrew, testing equipment and new tactics, and giving air experience to possible future RAF personnel in the affiliated youth organisations. It is logical to view first the upper structures of the RAF.

Overall control of the RAF is vested in the Air Force Board, subject, of course, to political directives from the government of the day. Beneath Board level are three Commands, two of which may be combined in the near future.

● **STRIKE COMMAND** (HQ: High Wycombe, Bucks) is responsible for all combat and operational support roles in all theatres, apart from Germany. Formed on 30 April 1968, it is commanded by an Air Chief Marshal who wears the dual 'hats' of AOC-in-C Strike Command (AOCinC STC) and C-in-C United Kingdom Air Forces (CIN-CUKAIR), the latter a NATO appointment. Since 10 April 1975, STC has been wholly committed to NATO as one of its four Major Subordinate Commands, although its HQ was not fully 'internationalised' with allied personnel (as is normal with a NATO HQ) until 1987. Most assets are assigned to NATO's Allied Command Europe, but some are earmarked for Supreme Allied Commander Atlantic and C-in-C Channel (that position is soon to be abolished). Under the *Options for Change* force reductions, STC is being cut from its 1990 peak of 800 aircraft and 49,000 military and 5,000 civilian personnel. It is divided into three Groups and several directly attached units:

● **No 1 Group** (HQ: Upavon, Wilts) administering over-land strike/attack, reconnaissance, transport, army support and aerial refuelling bases. Management of transport and refuelling aircraft (but not their bases) is actually undertaken at HQ Strike Command and not at Upavon.

● **No 11 Group** (HQ: Stanmore, London) which has all air defence assets, including interceptors and AEW aircraft.

● **No 18 Group** (HQ: Northwood, London) responsible for maritime patrol, maritime strike attack, SAR and target facilities.

● **MATO Military Air Traffic Organisation** (HQ: Uxbridge) No aircraft, although of Group status.

Direct reporting elements are the Central Tactics & Trials Organisation (formed 30 April 1968 and now at Boscombe Down) and overseas squadrons outside Germany. The latter are provided by Strike Command but controlled operationally by the local Headquarters of British Forces, all of which report directly to the tri-service Chief of Defence Staff. They are HQBF Belize, HQBF Cyprus, HQBF Falkland Islands, HQBF Gibraltar and HQBF Hong Kong.

HONG KONG

Following the reduction in size of RAF Germany during 1991-92, it is expected that this HQ will disband and become a numbered Group of Strike Command. At the same time, the status of the transport and tanker force (half way between High Wycombe and Upavon) will be regularised by assigning it a Group number, the administration still to be within Strike Command HQ (the Senior Air Staff Officer functioning as the Air Officer Commanding). Its assets are designated '1 Group-TT' in the listings below.

● **RAF GERMANY** (HQ: Rheindahlen) is contracting as a result of German unification in October 1990 and disbandment of the Warsaw Pact in 1991. It may be demoted to a Group and become a component of Strike Command. Aircraft of RAFG are one element of NATO's 2nd Allied Tactical Air Force (TWOATAF), of which the RAF officer leading RAFG is also commander. TWOATAF is the northern component of Allied Air Forces Central Europe (AAFCE), partnering FOURATAF. NATO plans to disband the 2nd and 4th ATAFs and control the smaller num-

ROYAL AIR FORCE GERMANY

ber of Allied units directly from AAFCE at Ramstein. Immediately before the reductions began, the Command operated five flying stations, the hospital at Wegberg, a weapons range at Nordhorn and No 431 MU, and additionally acted as parent unit for detachments to NATO HQs (SHAPE, AFCENT and AAFCE) and the NATO air combat range at Decimomannu, Sardinia.

● **SUPPORT COMMAND** (HQ: Brampton, Cambridgeshire) is tasked with all other tasks not mentioned above, ranging from flying training to storage of supplies. Its bases are listed later in this chapter.

Most squadrons can trace their ancestry to World War 1 — or before — and in the past few years have celebrated their 75th anniversaries. Numbering of Royal Flying Corps squadrons started at 1, but a second series for strategic bomber squadrons was begun in February 1917 at 100. When the

Royal Naval Air Service joined with the RAF on 1 April 1918 to form the RAF, its squadrons had 200 added to their numbers. The result is a group of maritime-related units currently between 201 and 208, whilst No 216 remembers No 16 Squadron, RNAS, by calling itself 'two-sixteen' squadron.

European escapee and Commonwealth squadrons of World War 2 were numbered 300-358 and 400-490, so when an unused number was required in 1966 for a joint RAF-Royal Navy unit, 360 was chosen. No 360 remains the RAF's youngest squadron. The 500 and 600 series were begun by Reservist and Auxiliary squadrons in the 1920s and 1930s and extended during World War 2. First to encroach upon the series previously reserved for the Auxiliaries was No 617 Squadron, the famed 'Dam Busters', which exist to this day. The highest number was No 695. Squadrons of Balloon command were numbered in the 900s, allowing for naval units in the 700s and

800s. Flights standardised on the 1300, 1400 and 1500 and 1600 series (followed by naval squadrons in the 1700s and 1800s) and continued into the 1900s for army air observation post units. Whereas most other types of unit have been numbered upwards from 1, Operational Conversion Units began at No 226 OCU, formed on 15 August 1946, following-on from OTUs between 1 and 200 and AFSs in the reserved block 201-225. Squadrons are formed and disbanded as required by re-equipment programmes and almost all have spent at least some time in limbo. Policy for re-forming units is broadly to select the disbanded squadron with the greatest accumulated service, although historical precedent is sometimes allowed influence, to the extent that famous fighter squadrons are perpetuated in that role whenever possible. The NATO forces build-up of the 1980s reached its culmination for the RAF on 1 January 1990 when No 13 Squadron was re-formed. With contraction now in vogue, it is most unlikely that any more numbers will be revived.

Indeed, to perpetuate long-serving squadrons made redundant by the run-down of RAF Germany, their 'number-plates' are being assigned to OCUs and FTSs. The practice is not new, having begun in 1955, but the principle is being extended. Hitherto, OCUs which would have put one or more squadrons into the front line (crewed by instructors) in wartime were assigned a Reserve Squadron number — usually called a 'shadow squadron' — and often applied the squadron's markings to their aircraft. OCUs which would split their aircraft and personnel to reinforce several existing squadrons have no requirement for a Reserve identity. This has changed with the latest batch of number allocations to such OCUs in 1991-92. Newer still is the 1992 assignment of fighter squadron numbers to components of Nos 4 and 7 FTSs.

The first part of the unit listing which follows comprises the operational units of Strike Command and RAF Germany. Data given includes unit number, base, attached command and group, current aircraft type and role. Badge data are given only in sufficient detail to differentiate squadrons operating the same aircraft type and should not be assumed to describe the complete insignia. 'Marking' indicates that a squadron's aircraft carry a device other than its badge.

Strike Command and RAF Germany

● **No 1 Squadron** Wittering (Strike/1 Group), Harrier GR5, battlefield air interdiction/close air support. Formed with balloons on 13 May 1912, No 1 became the world's first operational STO/VL squadron when converted to Harriers in 1969. The considerably upgraded Harrier GR5 was introduced in November 1988 and No 1 became operational with the variant 12 months later. Badge: a winged '1'.

● **No II Squadron** Marham (Strike/1 Group), Tornado GR1A, tactical reconnaissance and attack. Formed the same day as its predecessor, No II claims to be the oldest RAF unit equipped from the outset with aircraft. Tornados were received in September 1988 and the squadron moved from Germany to Marham on 3 December 1991. Badge: a Wake Knot.

● **No 3 Squadron** Gütersloh (RAFG), Harrier GR7, battlefield air interdiction/close air support. In Germany since April 1945, the squadron received Harriers in 1972 and was first in RAFG with the GR5 when it began to equip in March 1989. Replacement GR7s arrived from November 1990. Badge: a Cockatrice (dragon).

● **No IV Squadron** Gütersloh (RAFG), Harrier GR7, battlefield air interdiction/close air support. Having brought the first Harrier GR1s to Germany in 1970, No IV was first with the new GR7, acceptances of which began in September 1990. It will move to Laarbruch with No 3 Squadron in 1992-93. Badge: a lightning flash.

● **No 5 Squadron** Coningsby (Strike/11 Group), Tornado F3, air defence. Based mainly overseas with fighters until it became a Lightning unit at Binbrook in 1965, No 5 re-formed with Tornados on 1 January 1988 as the second squadron thus equipped. A joint No 5/29 Squadron unit was the first RAF combat component in Saudi Arabia after the invasion of Kuwait. Badge: a maple leaf.

● **No 6 Squadron** Coltishall (Strike/1 Group), Jaguar GR1A/T2A, battlefield and counter-air interdiction/close air support. Optimised for rapid overseas deployment as a Regional Reinforcement Squadron or in support of the Allied Command Europe Mobile Force, No 6 has flown Jaguars since October 1974. Marking: a winged can-opener.

● **No 7 Squadron** Odiham (Strike/1 Group), Chinook HC1B, helicopter support (plus one Gazelle HT3, liaison). After a career as diverse as bombing and provision of target facilities, No 7 re-formed at Odiham on 1 September 1982 as the home-based Chinook squadron, tasked primarily with supporting the army in medium-lift roles. Badge: the constellation of Ursa Major.

● **No 8 Squadron** Waddington (Strike/11 Group), Sentry AEW1, airborne early warning. NATO's last piston-engined front-line aircraft were withdrawn on 30 June 1990 when No 8 disbanded as a Shackleton unit at Lossiemouth. It re-formed at Waddington the following day with long-awaited new equipment. Crews are provided by the co-located Sentry Training Squadron (formed 1 June 1990). Badge: an Arabian dagger.

● **No IX Squadron** Brüggen (RAFG), Tornado GR1, strike/attack. A bomber unit since 1924, this squadron re-formed at Honington on 1 June 1982 as the first operational user of the Tornado GR1 and joined RAFG on 1 October 1986. Badge: a bat.

● **No 10 Squadron** Brize Norton (Strike/1 Group), VC10 C1, strategic transport. Appropriately, No 10 Squadron equipped with VC10s in July 1966 and is engaged in flying personnel and freight throughout the world on scheduled and unscheduled services. Eight of its 13 aircraft are being converted to C1(K) tankers with underwing pods. Badge: a winged arrow.

● **No XI Squadron** Leeming (Strike/11 Group), Tornado F3, air defence. The first F3 squadron at Leeming formed on 1 July 1988 and became operational on 1 November. Its assignment is to forward operations in defence of maritime assets, for which purpose it would be based at Stornoway in wartime. Badge: two eagles.

● **No 12 Squadron** Lossiemouth (Strike/18 Group), Buccaneer S2B, Hunter T7/T7B, maritime strike/attack. Formed on 1 October 1969 as the RAF's first Buccaneer squadron, No 12 began moving to Lossiemouth on 4 August 1980, completing the move in October, and is now operational with weapons including the BAe Sea Eagle anti-ship missile. It will convert to Tornados in the same role during 1993. Hunters are used for pilot's instrument rating checks. Badge: a fox's mask.

● **No 13 Squadron** Honington (Strike/1 Group), Tornado GR1A, tactical reconnaissance/conventional attack. This former Canberra PR9 squadron was revived on 1 January 1990 as the second and last Tornado recce unit. Transfer to Marham to join the similarly-tasked No II Squadron is due before June 1993. Badge: a lynx's face.

● **No 14 Squadron** Brüggen (RAFG), Tornado GR1, strike/attack. In Germany since 1946, the squadron has held its current role with Canberras, Phantoms, Jaguars and (from 1 November 1985) Tornados. Badge: a red cross on a white, winged disc.

● **No XV (Reserve) Squadron** Honington (Strike/1 Group), Tornado GR1, training. Disbanded as a Tornado squadron at Laarbruch on 18 December 1991, the unit returned to the air on 1 April 1992 as the 'shadow' identity of the Tornado Weapons Conversion Unit, displacing No 45 (Reserve) Squadron.

● **No 16 (Reserve) Squadron** Lossiemouth (Strike/1 Group), Jaguar GR1A/T2A, training. First of the Tornado GR1 squadrons to disappear, No 16 disbanded at Laarbruch on 11 September 1991. On 1 November 1991, No 226 OCU was given the 'shadow' identity of No 16. Markings: 'The Saint' and crossed keys.

● **No 17 Squadron** Brüggen (RAFG), Tornado GR1, strike/attack. No 17 Squadron — 'The Black Knights' — has been in Germany since 1956 and in the strike/attack role from 1970. Phantoms and then Jaguars gave way to Tornados on 1 March 1985. Badge: a red gauntlet.

● **No 18 Squadron** Gütersloh (RAFG) Chinook HC1B, helicopter support. No 18 gained helicopter experience in Germany for most of the years between 1965 and 1980. Re-formed at Odiham on 24 February 1982, it was diverted for service in the Falklands War two months later and did not begin returning to Germany until 21 April 1983, the official consolidation date being 6 August 1983. Half the Chinooks will transfer to Laarbruch in 1993, joined by half a squadron of Pumas. Badge: Pegasus.

● **No 19 (Reserve) Squadron** Disbanded with Phantom FGR2s at Wildenrath 9 January 1992. On 1 April 1992, No 2 TWU passed from No 11 Group of Strike Command to Support Command, simultaneously forming two new 'shadow' squadrons to replace existing components. No 19 Squadron now partners Nos 79 and 92 Squadrons in operating Hawks within the re-titled No 7 FTS at Chivenor. Badge: a dolphin.

● **No 20 (Reserve) Squadron** Wittering (Strike/1 Group) Harrier T4/T4A/GR3/GR5, training. Disbanded as a Tornado GR1 unit at Laarbruch in May 1992, the squadron was assigned to No 233 OCU on 1 September 1992. Badge: an eagle.

● **No 22 Squadron** St Mawgan (Strike/18 Group) Wessex HC2, search and rescue. Officially assigned to rescuing downed airmen, the RAF's SAR force is heavily involved with civilian duties. No 22 Squadron has four flights: 'A' (Chivenor), 'B' (Leuchars), 'C' (Valley) and 'E' (Coltishall). First Wessex arrived in 1976, and the last Whirlwind was withdrawn in 1981. Badge: Greek letter 'pi' over a Maltese Cross.

● **No 23 Squadron** Leeming (Strike/11 Group) Tornado F3, air defence. A Phantom squadron since 1975, No 23 defended the Falkland Islands from 1983 until 1 November 1988 when it became a Tornado operator. One of the RAF's most famous fighter squadrons, it was declared operational on 1 August 1989. Badge: an eagle.

● **No 24 Squadron** Lyneham (Strike/1 Group-TT) Hercules C1/C1(K)/C3, transport. No 24 has a long tradition of transport operations, including VIP/VVIP flying during World War 2. On 5 January 1968 it left its Hastings at Colerne and moved to Lyneham to begin receiving Hercules. Its specialities are route flying and aerial tanking, for which it detaches crews to No 1312 Flight in the Falkland Islands. Aircraft are taken from the Lyneham pool as required for individual tasks.

● **No 25 Squadron** Leeming (Strike/11 Group) Tornado F3, air defence. As one of the RAF's traditional fighter units, No 25 was in the less colourful world of surface-to-air missiles between 1963 and 1 October 1989, when its 'number-plate' was transferred to a Tornado squadron forming at Leeming. It became operational on 1 January 1990. Badge: a hawk perched on a gauntlet.

● **No 27 Squadron** Marham (Strike/1 Group) Tornado GR1, strike/attack. A Vulcan squadron between 1961 and 1982 — the last nine years in maritime radar reconnaissance — No 27 was the RAF's third operational Tornado GR1 squadron when reformed at Marham on 1 May 1983. With No 617, it is the RAF component of SACEUR's Strategic Reserve (Air). Badge: an elephant.

● **No 28 Squadron** Sek Kong (Strike/direct reporting) Wessex HC2, army support. This unit has been Hong Kong's helicopter squadron since 1 March 1968 and was resident in the colony with fighters between 1949 and 1966. It began replacing Whirlwinds by the current equipment in January 1972. Helicopters are used to transport border security patrols, assist the local police and undertake the regular tasks of SAR and medical evacuation. Since 1917 it has spent three months (non-operational) in the UK. Badge: Pegasus.

● **No 29 Squadron** Coningsby (Strike/11 Group) Tornado F3, air defence. A dozen years with Phantoms ended for No 29 Squadron with disbandment on the last day of March 1987. On 1 May 1987 it reformed at Coningsby as the first Tornado F3 squadron and became operational on 1 November. It is assigned to SACLANT for support of maritime operations and earmarked for deployment outside the NATO area. Badge: an eagle preying on a buzzard.

● **No 30 Squadron** Lyneham (Strike/1 Group-TT) Hercules C1/C1(K)/C3, transport. Re-formed on 1 May 1968 at Fairford, No 30 equipped with Hercules and transferred to its present base on 24 September 1971. Principal duties are route-flying and provision of air-refuelling crews for No 1312 Flight in the Falkland Islands. Equipment is drawn from the Lyneham pool and does not bear squadron markings.

● **No 31 Squadron** Brüggen (RAFG) Tornado GR1, strike/attack. having been the first RAF squadron in India (December 1915), this unit led a varied career in army co-operation, transport and reconnaissance until it received strike/attack Phantoms at Brüggen in 1971, followed by Jaguars in 1976. These were exchanged for Tornados on 1 November 1984, No 31 becoming the first thus equipped in the Brüggen wing. Badge: a five-pointed star.

● **No 32 Squadron** Northolt (Strike/1 Group-TT), Andover C1/CC2, BAe 125 C1/C2/C3, Islander CC2 and Gazelle HT3, communications. On 3 February 1969 the No 32 'number-plate' was transferred from a Canberra B15 unit at Akrotiri to the Metropolitan Communications Squadron. Responsible for carrying VIPs and non-royal VVIPs, the squadron had Andovers in its equipment when formed and added BAe 125s from 1971 and Gazelles from 1976. The Islander, which has a secondary surveillance role, was delivered in December 1991. Badge: a hunting horn.

● **No 33 Squadron** Odiham (Strike/1 Group) Puma HC1, helicopter support. On reformation at Odiham on 14 June 1971, the squadron equipped with Pumas, which it uses to provide tactical support for the army, including short-notice deployment overseas. Badge: a hart's head.

● **No 38 (Reserve) Squadron** St Mawgan (Strike/18 Group) Nimrod MR2, training. The traditions of a long-established maritime squadron are maintained as a 'shadow' identity of No 236 OCU, bestowed in July 1970. The unit moves to Kinloss before the end of 1992.

● **No 41 Squadron** Coltishall (Strike/1 Group) Jaguar GR1A/T2A, tactical reconnaissance/battlefield air interdiction. Following the adoption of video reconnaissance by the Tornado GR1A, No 41's Jaguars are the only RAF tactical recce assets using 'wet film' photography. Carrying one of two types of camera pod, the squadron is assigned to the Allied Command Europe Mobile Force (Air) and has a secondary attack role. Badge: a Cross of Lorraine.

● **No 42 Squadron** Disbanded in August 1992 having been a Nimrod MR2 unit at St Mawgan.

● **No 43 Squadron** Leuchars (Strike/11 Group) Tornado F3, air defence. The 'Fighting Cocks' have been at Leuchars since September 1969, when formed with Phantom FG1s diverted from naval contracts. Tornados began arriving in September 1989 and the squadron was declared operational on 1 July 1990. Badge: a fighting cock.

● **No 45 (Reserve) Squadron** Disbanded on 31 March 1992 as the 'shadow' of the TWCU at Honington.

● **No 47 Squadron** Lyneham (Strike/1 Group-TT) Hercules C1/C3, transport. Having been the first squadron to operate the Hastings (and flown in the Berlin Airlift) and Beverley, this unit has rightfully remained in the transport role. Re-formed with Hercules at Fairford on 25 February 1968 it moved to Lyneham on 1 February 1971 and specialises in short-range tactical work, including carriage of 'special forces'. No squadron markings applied to aircraft of the Lyneham pool.

● **No 51 Squadron** Wyton (Strike/18 Group) Nimrod R1, electronic reconnaissance. On 21 August 1958, No 192 squadron was renumbered at Watton, but moved to its current base on 1 April 1963. Formerly equipped with Comets and Canberras, it flew its first mission with one of three new Nimrods in May 1974. The aircraft are equipped with antennae to gather details of other forces' radio/radar frequencies and procedures (the 'electronic order of battle') and have played a vital, but unannounced role in the Falklands and Gulf Wars. Badge: a goose.

● **No 54 Squadron** Coltishall (Strike/1 Group) Jaguar GR1A/T2A, battlefield air interdiction/close air support. No 54 is a renowned fighter squadron which re-formed with Jaguars at Lossiemouth on 29 March 1974 and was transferred to Coltishall on 8 August that year. Like the other Coltishall units (Nos 6 and 41) it is equipped to bolster the NATO flanks in wartime — in this instance classed as a Regional Reinforcement Squadron. Badge: a rampant lion.

● **No 55 Squadron** Marham (Strike/1 Group-TT) Victor K2, aerial refuelling. No 55 formed on 1 September 1960 as a Victor B1 bomber squadron but transferred to refuelling in 1965 — in which year it moved from Honington to Marham. Re-equipment with the K2 version officially took place on 1 July 1975. Battle honours include the Falklands and Gulf Wars. Disbandment is due in October 1993. Badge: forearm holding a spear.

● **No 56 Squadron** Disbanded at Wattisham in September 1992 as a Phantom FGR2 unit, having stood-down on 30 June 1992.

● **No 60 Squadron** Disbanded at Wildenrath on 31 March 1992 as an Andover C1/C1(PR)/CC2 unit.

● **No 63 (Reserve) Squadron** This 'shadow' of No 2 TWU disbanded on 31 March 1992, having been replaced by No 19 Squadron.

● **No 64 (Reserve) Squadron** Disbanded at Leuchars on 31 January 1991 as a 'shadow' of Phantom FGR2-equipped No 228 OCU.

● **No 65 (Reserve) Squadron** Coningsby (Strike/11 Group) Tornado F3, training. Re-formed on 1 January 1987 to 'shadow' No 229 OCU. Badge: a lion.

● **No 70 Squadron** Lyneham (Strike/1 Group-TT) Hercules C1/C3, transport. Large bombers and transports have equipped this squadron for 70 years, the most recent in November 1970 when Hercules were received in Cyprus before a move to Lyneham on 15 January 1975. The main duty of No 70 is short-range tactical transport, including cargo drops by parachute-extraction. Aircraft carry no unit markings.

● **No 72 Squadron** Aldergrove (Strike/1 Group) Wessex HC2, helicopter support. Once a distinguished fighter squadron, No 72 re-equipped with helicopters in 1961 when Belvederes were received. The present Wessex arrived in 1964 and the squadron took-up residence at Aldergrove on 12 November 1981. It is possible that the squadron will be half equipped with surplus

Pumas from Germany in 1993. Badge: a swift.

● **No 74 Squadron** Wattisham (Strike/11 Group) Phantom FRG2, air defence. 'The Tigers' are one of the RAF's best-known fighter squadrons. Their current commission began on 1 July 1984 when they began collecting 15 F-4J(UK) versions of the Phantom bought second-hand from the USA. These were replaced by the Phantom FGR2 in January 1991 (first sortie on 17th), but the squadron stood down from NATO on 30 September 1992 and disbanded soon afterwards. Badge: a tiger's face.

● **No 78 Squadron** Mount Pleasant (Strike/Direct reporting) Chinook HC1B and Puma HC1, helicopter support and SAR. Assigned to support of the Falkland Islands garrison this unusual squadron is staffed by personnel on rotation from Europe and has only two of each kind of helicopter, making it the RAF's smallest unit of squadron status. It formed on 22 May 1986 from Nos 1310 (Chinook) and 1564 (Sea King) Flights. Badge: an heraldic tiger.

● **No 79 (Reserve) Squadron** Disbanded when No 1 TWU (Hawk T1A at Brawdy) closed on 31 August 1992, but was due to re-form as the third component of No 7 FTS at Chivenor, still with Hawks. Marking: an arrowhead.

● **No 84 Squadron** Akrotiri (Strike/Direct reporting) Wessex HC5C, SAR/support helicopter. No 84 Squadron formed at Akrotiri on 17 January 1972 with Whirlwinds and converted to Wessex HC2s in March 1982. However, in June 1984 it began receiving ex-Navy Wessex HU5s, five of which are currently used. The squadron provides local SAR cover and transports security patrols within the UK Sovereign Base Area in western Cyprus. Badge: a scorpion.

● **No 85 Squadron** Disbanded on 10 July 1991 as a Bloodhound SAM squadron at West Raynham and Wattisham.

● **No 92 (Reserve) Squadron** Disbanded on 5 July 1991 as a Phantom FGR2 squadron at Wildenrath. It re-formed at Chivenor on 1 April 1992 as a 'shadow' squadron of No 7 FTS. Badge: a cobra.

● **No 100 Squadron** Wyton (Strike/18 Group) Hawk T1/T1A, target facilities. This former bomber squadron, formed 11 February 1917, was established in the target facilities role on 1 February 1972, flying adapted Canberra bombers. At Wyton since 5 January 1982, it began a major change of equipment when the first of 12 replacement Hawks arrived on 5 September 1991. It

recommissioned as a Hawk unit on 6 January 1992. Badge: a skull and cross-bones.

● **No 101 Squadron** Brize Norton (Strike/1 Group-TT) VC10 K2/K3, aerial refuelling. No 101 left the bomber world when re-formed on 1 May 1984 to receive tanker conversions of the VC10 airliner. Its past distinctions have included being the first operator of the Canberra (May 1951). Badge: a lion.

● **No 111 Squadron** Leuchars (Strike/11 Group) Tornado F3, air defence. 'Treble One' has a long history of fighter operations, perpetuated on 1 May 1990 when it re-formed with Tornado F3s, to become operational six months later. The unit has been at Leuchars since 3 November 1975, when it was an operator of Phantoms. Badge: a Palestine Cross.

● **No 115 Squadron** Benson (Strike/1 Group) Andover E3/E3A, navigation aids calibration. No 115 has been involved with calibration duties since 1958 and began receiving its present equipment in November 1976. Fitting-out of aircraft took some time, and so the last Argosy E1 did not depart until January 1978. A move to Benson took pace on 7 January 1983. The Andover's wartime role is airborne radio relay. Badge: a hand holding a tiller.

● **No 120 Squadron** Kinloss (Strike/18 Group) Nimrod MR2, maritime patrol. Associated with maritime operations since 1941, No 120 moved to Kinloss with Shackletons on 1 April 1959 and began receiving Nimrods in September 1970, using the MR1 version for some 10 years. Aircraft are pooled with Nos 120 and 206 Squadrons (and No 236 OCU from late-1992) and so wear no squadron markings.

● **No 151 (Reserve) Squadron** Disbanded at Chivenor on 1 April 1992 when No 92 Squadron replaced it as a 'shadow' of No 7 FTS.

● **No 201 Squadron** Kinloss (Strike/18 Group) Nimrod MR2, maritime patrol. No 1 Squadron of the Royal Naval Air Service was renumbered No 201 Squadron on formation of the RAF on 1 April 1918. Its maritime associations continue to this day — specifically at Kinloss since 14 March 1965. Shackletons were exchanged for Nimrod MR1s from June 1970 onwards and the squadron accepted the RAF's first MR2 conversion on 23 August 1979. No squadron markings are worn.

● **No 202 Squadron** Boulmer (Strike/18 Group) Sea King HAR3, SAR. Responsible for long-range, all-weather SAR around the UK

Above:
Pictured shortly before the conversion of No 100 Squadron to Hawks, one of the unit's Canberra PR7s flies in formation with a Tornado F3 from No 23 Squadron.
Paul Jackson

Below:
There are a few far-flung corners of the world left for the RAF, including Belize, where Harrier GR3s of No 1417 Flight are based. *RAF*

coast (with No 22 Squadron's Wessex providing the short-range, limited operational element), No 202 re-equipped from Whirlwinds to Sea Kings, beginning with its Lossiemouth detachment in August 1978. Its organisation (since a reassignment of flights in mid-1988) is now 'A' to 'E' Flights at Boulmer, Brawdy, Manston, Lossiemouth and Leconfield, respectively. The HQ was at Finningley between 1 September 1976 and 1 October 1992. Badge: a mallard.

● **No 206 Squadron** Kinloss (Strike/18 Group) Nimrod MR2, maritime patrol. Moving to Kinloss with Shackletons on 7 July 1965, the squadron converted to Nimrod MR1s from November 1970 and to the MR2 10 years later. No squadron markings are carried.

● **No 208 Squadron** Lossiemouth (Strike/18 Group) Buccaneer S2B and Hunter T7/T8, maritime strike/attack. Formed at Honington on 1 July 1974 as a Buccaneer operator, No 208 moved to Lossiemouth on 1 July 1983. Its duties include laser-guided bombing, which was used to good effect in the Gulf War of 1991. The squadron will disband late in 1993, following its replacement by No 617 Squadron (Tornado GR1). Badge: a winged eye.

● **No 216 Squadron** Brize Norton (Strike/1 Group-TT) TriStar K1/KC1/C2, tanker/transport. Despite the tanker capabilities of most of its nine TriStars the squadron is principally involved with transporting freight and personnel. Over half its work is unscheduled support of exercises and deployments. It formed in its present role on 1 November 1984 using only passenger variants. The first tanker (K1) was received on 25 March 1986; the first KC1 on 9 December 1988; and first C2 on 18 September 1985. Badge: an eagle holding a bomb.

● **No 230 Squadron** Gütersloh (RAFG) Puma HC1, helicopter support. In October 1971, Pumas began arriving to replace Whirlwinds in No 230 Squadron. Still in the army support role, it moved from Odiham to Gütersloh on 14 October 1980 and resumed operational status in Germany on 1 December that year. The squadron is expected to break-up in 1993, with part of its helicopters going to Laarbruch and the remainder to Aldergrove. Badge: a tiger.

● **No 234 (Reserve) Squadron** Disbanded with closure of No 1 TWU (Brawdy with Hawk T1A) on 31 August 1992. (The longest-serving 'shadow' squadron, No 234 formed in No 229 OCU at Chivenor in November 1958.)

● **No 360 Squadron** Wyton (Strike/18 Group) Canberra T17/T17A, target facilities/jamming. The RAF's youngest squadron formed for the first time on 1 April 1966 and shortly afterwards received Canberra T17s equipped to jam electronic transmissions to give operators practice in working in the face of enemy jamming. Uniquely, it contains a 25 per cent naval staff and every fourth CO is a RN officer. One Canberra E15 was added early in 1992. Disbandment is expected late in 1993 with reallocation of the task to civilian contractors flying converted executive jets. Badge: a moth on Neptune's trident.

● **No 617 Squadron** Marham (Strike/1 Group) Tornado GR1, strike/attack. 'The Dam Busters' formed on 21 March 1943 and made history on 16 May that year with a raid on German dams using surface-skimming mines. The present period of operations began with re-formation on 1 January 1983 and formal commissioning on 16 May 1983. Assigned to SACEUR's Strategic Reserve (Air) in the nuclear strike role (with co-located No 27 Squadron), the unit will move to Lossiemouth in October 1993 and equip its Tornados with Sea Eagle missiles.

FLIGHTS

When deployment of a full squadron is not demanded by circumstances, between two and four aircraft are assigned to a numbered Flight, which reports directly to Strike Command.

● **No 1312 Flight**

Mount Pleasant	Hercules C1(K)	Tanker/maritime surveillance	Badge: none carried

● **No 1417 Flight**

Belize City	Harrier GR3	Close air support	Badge: a sailfish

● **No 1435 Flight**

Mount Pleasant	Phantom FGR2*	Air defence	Marking: a Maltese Cross

● **No 1563 Flight**

Belize City	Puma HC1	Helicopter support	Badge: a snake's head

*Expected to receive Tornado F3s in June 1992

OPERATIONAL CONVERSION UNITS

The role of an OCU is to convert pilots and other aircrew to a specific type of first-line aircraft and train experienced personnel as Qualified Instructors both for their own use and to be resident with squadrons. In wartime, OCUs would join the order of battle with instructors flying their aircraft, either by activating their 'shadow' squadrons or splitting the OCU to reinforce two or more existing squadrons. Nos 236, 241 and 242 OCUs borrow aircraft from a central pool. Associated Reserve Squadrons, where assigned, are given in the fourth column.

● **No 226 OCU**	Lossiemouth	Jaguar GR1A/T2A	No 16 (Reserve) Squadron; Badges: a torch & quiver (226) and a 'Saint' and cross-keys (16)
● **No 228 OCU***			Disbanded 31 January 1991; (was Phantom at Leuchars)
● **No 229 OCU**	Coningsby	Tornado F3	No 65 (Reserve) Squadron; Badges: a torch & sword (229) and a lion (65)
● **No 231 OCU**			Disbanded 31 December 1990; (Was Canberra at Wyton)
● **No 233 OCU**	Wittering	Harrier T4/T4A/GR3/GR5	No 20 (Reserve) Squadron; Badge: a wildcat's face**
● **No 236 OCU**	Kinloss	Nimrod MR2	No 38 (Reserve) Squadron; No insignia carried
● **No 237 OCU**			Disbanded 1 October 1991; (was Buccaneer at Lossiemouth)
● **No 240 OCU**	Odiham	Chinook HC1B/Puma HC1; Badge: a hummingbird	
● **No 241 OCU**	Brize Norton	TriStar K1/KC1/K2;VC10 C1/K2/K3; No insignia carried	
	Benson	BAe 146 CC2	
● **No 242 OCU**	Lyneham	Hercules C1/C3/C1(K); No insignia carried	

* Reserve Squadron was No 64.
** No 20 Squadron insignia to be added in September 1992; Badge: an eagle clutching a sword before a rising sun

TACTICAL WEAPONS UNITS

Pilots who learned to fly at FTSs until recently gained basic weapon and tactics skills at a TWU. No 1 TWU formed on 2 September 1974 at Brawdy (known as simply TWU until 1 August 1978) but disbanded on 31 August 1992. Its two Hawk T1A shadow squadrons were Nos 79 and 234. TWU administration was by No 11 Group because of the wartime commitment to day air defence with Sidewinder-armed aircraft. The standard course was 54 hours (including 36 solo) over 16 weeks. No 79 Squadron formerly provided the non-standard training, such as refresher courses (33-53 hours, as required) and Qualified Weapons Instructor Courses (56 hours). In 1992 the RAF adopted a revised training scheme combining the old FTS and TWU courses in a new, 100-hour joint flying/weapons training course. No 4 FTS added armament training and No 2 TWU joined Support Command on 1 April 1992, shortly to become No 7 FTS with an added commitment to pure flying training.

● **No 1 TWU**	Disbanded 31 August 1992
● **No 2 TWU**	To Support Command 1 April 1992 as No 7 FTS (Designate)

OTHER TRAINING UNITS

● **Andover Training Flight**	Benson	Andover	Aircraft on loan; (Strike/1 Group-TT)
● **Canberra Training Flight**	Wyton	Canberra T4	No insignia; (Strike/18 Group)
● **Phantom Training Flight**			Disbanded 30 December 1991 at Wattisham
● **SAR Training Unit**	Valley	Wessex HC2	On loan from No 22 Squadron*; (Strike/18 Group)
● **Sea King Training Flight**	Culdrose†	Sea King HAR3	On loan from No 202 Squadron*; (Strike/18 Group)
● **Sentry Training Squadron**	Waddington	Sentry AEW1	On loan from No 8 Squadron*(Strike/11 Group)
● **Trinational Tornado Training Establishment**	Cottesmore	Tornado GR1/IDS	Badge: 'TTTE' within a dart, plus either a Tornado in plan ('C' Sqn) or embellished letters 'A', 'B' or 'S'. (Strike/1 Group)
● **Tornado Weapons Conversion Unit**	Honington	Tornado GR1	No XV (Reserve) Squadron; Badge: a crown and sword (TWCU) — XV to be applied. (Strike/1 Group)

*Correctly, the helicopters are 'owned' by the SAR Wing at St Mawgan and the Sentries by Waddington's Engineering Wing.
†St Mawgan from April 1993.

MISCELLANEOUS UNITS

● **Berlin Station Fight**	Gatow	Chipmunk T10	(RAFG)
● **Canberra Training and Standardisation Flight**	Wyton	Canberra T4	(Strike/18 Group)
● **Electronic Warfare Avionic Unit**	Wyton	as required	(Strike/18 Group)
● **No 1 Photographic Reconnaissance Unit**	Wyton	Canberra PR9/PR7	(Strike/18 Group)
● **Strike/Attack Operational Evaluation Unit***	Boscombe Down	Tornado GR1/ Harrier GR7 Jaguar T2A	(Strike/Direct reporting)
● **Tornado F3 Operational Evaluation Unit***	Coningsby	Tornado F3	(Strike/direct reporting)
● **The Queen's Flight**	Benson	BAe 146 CC2/ Wessex HCC4	(Strike/1 Group-TT)

*Both units are part of the Central Tactics and Trials Organization and both carry its badge of three swords in a 'Y' pattern.

Non-flying units include:
● **No 26 Signals Unit**	Berlin (RAFG)
● **No 144 Signals Unit** (Strike Command Mobile Radar Reserve)	Ty Croes, Gwynedd
● **No 7 Signals Unit** (radar site)	Byron Heights, Falkland Islands
● **No 751 Signals Unit** (radar site)	Mount Alice, Falkland Islands
● **No 303 Signals Unit** (radar site)	Mount Kent, Falkland Islands

SUPPORT COMMAND

Unlike its Strike equivalent, Support Command is not divided into Groups of differing functions, but so diverse are its activities that they are classified under three headings. Below the Air Marshal designated as AOC-in-C for the whole of the Command are three Air Vice Marshals: AOC Training Units, AOC Maintenance Units and AOC Directly Administered Units, each responsible for administering the activities of Support Command coming within their area of responsibility. These are covered in detail below.

Support Command has 23,000 uniformed personnel — one-third of the RAFs total — plus 10,000 civilians. In addition it is responsible for 3,000 civilians working on USAF bases in the UK, 10,000 people under training for all sections of the RAF, and other administrative staff in the MoD. Total RAF strength is being reduced from 83,200 personnel to 75,000 over the next few years. The quoted figures are for trained personnel, excluding recruits under instruction and comprise 12,200 male and 1,000 female officers, 64,000 airmen and 5,000 airwomen. About 850 of the RAF's 1,700 aircraft are with Support Command at any time: the fleet of 400 training aircraft, plus those of all three Commands undergoing servicing, or in storage.

Despite its small budget (about £800 million of the £23,000 million defence allocation) Support Command operates 46 major and 167 minor units which are invaluable to the operations of the RAF's 'sharp end'. The diversity of services includes recruiting at 75 town offices in the UK; initial training; electrical and mechanical services; storage, supply and distribution of equipment, fuel and gases; communications; and medical provisions. In 1991, Support Command formed the Defence Supply Agency which is reorganising the maintenance units so that they can compete for work in the civilian sector when they have surplus capacity.

TRAINING UNITS

● Flying Training Schools

Flying activities of Support Command include training of prospective pilots up to 'wings' standard, shortly after which they will normally transfer to Strike Command to specialise in a particular aircraft type at an OCU (prefixed by a weapons course at the same FTS for combat pilots). Prospective pilots arrive at an FTS from one of three directions:

1. University Air Squadron. Those intending to make a long-term career in the RAF will have received a university grant from the RAF and flown 100 or so hours on Bulldogs by the time of leaving.

2. Flying Scholarship. Approximately 30 hours at a civilian flying school, up to civil licence standard, paid by the RAF.

3. Direct Entry. No previous flying experience and intending to take a short-term flying commission. Candidates are given 63 hours in Chipmunks of the EFTS at Swinderby.

In addition, however, all will first have passed through the Officer & Aircrew Selection Centre at Biggin Hill.

Conversion of pilot FTSs to the Jet Provost to Tucano is virtually complete. Flying Scholarship trainees take the Tucano 'Long Course' of 146hr, the others, the 'Short Course' lasting 130hr (university graduates at Cranwell), the goal being fast-jet flying (known as Group 1). Those assessed as not suitable for this most demanding group are moved from the Tucano course earlier. Multi-engined aircraft students (Group 2) relinquish the Tucano after 140hr (123 on the short course) and join the METS (Multi-Engine Training Squadron) at No 6 FTS, Finningley to fly 50hr in eight weeks on Jetstreams. Helicopter trainees (Group 3) leave Tucano at 63½hr (49½ 'short') for No 2 FTS and fly 80hr on Gazelles and 65hr on Wessex in 28 weeks. Group 1, meanwhile, will have had 75hr in 23 weeks on No 4 FTS Hawks.

The Central Flying School — the world's oldest flying school (formed 1912) — trains flying instructors and watches over flying standards throughout the RAF. No 6 FTS is also responsible for navigators, air engineers, air electronics officers and loadmasters. Finningley will replace Jet Provosts by a combination of Tucanos and Hawks in 1992-93. No 1 FTS/RNEFTS Bulldogs give 60hr of tuition to prospective naval pilots. The last Jet Provosts are being used by the Refresher Flying Flight (RFF) at Church Fenton for the benefit of pilots returning to flying after a desk-job.

● **Central Flying School**

Scampton	Tucano T1, Bulldog T1, (Jet Provost being withdrawn)/ Chipmunk T10 (on loan)/Hawk T1/T1A ('Red Arrows')	Marking: CFS arms
Det: Shawbury	Gazelle HT3	
Det: Valley	Hawk T1	
Det: Syerston	Vigilant T1/Valiant T1/Viking T1	

● **Elementary Flying Training School**

Swinderby   Chipmunk T10 — Marking: eagle and EFTS

● **No 1 FTS**

Linton-on-Ouse Jet Provost T3A/T5A (Tucano 1992) — Marking: '1 FTS'
  Det: Topcliffe   Bulldog T1 (RNEFTS)

● **No 2 FTS**

Shawbury   Gazelle HT3/Wessex HC2 — Marking: nil

● **No 3 FTS**

Cranwell   Tucano T1 — Marking: blue fuselage band

● **No 4 FTS**

Valley   Hawk T1/T1A — Marking: pyramid and palm tree. Plus Nos 56 and 74 (Reserve) Squadrons

● **No 6 FTS**

Finningley   Dominie T1/Jet Provost T5A/Jetstream T1 (METS) — Marking: RAF Finningley badge

● **No 7 FTS**

Church Fenton Tucano T1 (Disbands 1992)/Jet Provost T5A (RFF) — Marking: 'CF'

● **No 7 FTS**

Chivenor   Hawk T1/T1A (ex-No 2 TWU 1992)/ — Marking: Nos 19, 79 and 92 (Reserve) Squadrons

---

UNIVERSITY AIR SQUADRONS

Administered since 1971 by HQ UAS at Cranwell, UASs date back to October 1925 when units were formed at Oxford and Cambridge. London UAS was established in 1935 and 21 more in 1941. Some consolidation has taken place, and some UASs renamed to allow for an expanded catchment. Replacement of Chipmunks by Bulldogs began in September 1973 and ended in March 1975. Four or five aircraft is the usual complement, but London UAS has 10. Permanent RAF staff are assisted by members of the RAF Volunteer Reserve in these RAuxAF units.

● **Aberdeen, Dundee & St Andrews UAS**	Leuchars	Badge: lion holding a tower
● **Birmingham UAS**	Cosford	Badge: a double-headed lion
● **Bristol UAS**	Filton	Badge: a galleon
● **Cambridge UAS**	Cambridge	Badge: a lion
● **East Lowlands UAS**	Edinburgh	Badge: open book and white cross
● **East Midlands UAS**	Newton	Badge: a quiver of arrows
● **Glasgow & Strathclyde UAS**	Glasgow	Badge: a dove and sword
● **Liverpool UAS**	Woodvale	Badge: a cormorant and book
● **London UAS**	Benson	Badge: a globe and open book
● **Manchester UAS**	Woodvale	Badge: a sparrowhawk and snake
● **Northumbrian UAS**	Leeming	Badge: a white cross
● **Oxford UAS**	Benson	Badge: open book and crossed sword and staff
● **Queens UAS**	Sydenham	Badge: a winged torch
● **Southampton UAS**	Lee-on-Solent	Badge: a stag and pillar
● **U Wales AS**	St Athan	Badge: dragon and open book
● **Yorkshire UAS**	Finningley	Badge: white rose and open book

Above:
Nimrod squadrons keep watch on the furtive movements of submarines. Watching the position of plots on the computerised main display screen of an MR2 is 1st Navigator/tactical co-ordinator Flt Lt Rory Slater of No 201 Squadron assisted by 2nd Navigator Flt Lt Bruce Hargrave (nearest). *Paul Jackson*

Below:
University Air Squadrons have existed since 1925 and provided initial flying training to a high proportion of the RAF's greatest leaders. The 21st century's air marshals now fly Bulldog T1s. *Paul Jackson*

HEADQUARTERS AIR CADETS

Situated at Newton and commanded by an Air Commodore, HQAC administers the Air Training Corps and provides support to the RAF section of the Combined Cadet Corps, which is organised on a school basis. There are currently 40,000 cadets aged between 13 and 20 in 925 squadrons and 97 detached flights of this voluntary organisation, from which the RAF receives some 35% of all its regular entrants, and 50 per cent of officers. The ATC is the world's largest glider training organisation, but cadets also fly regularly in Chipmunks. Additionally, the Corps allocates annually over 300 Flying Scholarships (30 flying hours at a civilian school), 50 navigation scholarships (10hr), 800 flight-deck flights on civil airliners and other aircraft and 70 RAF overseas flights. The ATC operates 49 Chipmunks, one Bulldog, 53 Vigilant T1 power-assisted sailplanes, 97 Viking T1s, four Valiant T1s and two Janus Cs.

VOLUNTEER GLIDING SCHOOLS

These have a strength of either three Vigilants or between five and seven Vikings; only Air Cadets' Central Gliding School operates Janus and Valiant types, although these may be flown from locations other than Syerston. The first two digits of the VGS number refer to the long-defunct Nos 61-64 and 66 Groups of RAF Home Command in which particular schools were located. Survivors of the original schools, numbered 1 GS-203 GS, were renumbered in this system in 1955 and those formed subsequently have followed its regional plan. The ATC is now divided into seven home regions:

● **Central & East Region**	(ex part of No 61 Group)
● **London & South-East Region**	(ex part of No 61 Group)
● **South-West Region**	(ex No 62 Group)
● **Welsh Region**	(ex part of No 63 Group)
● **North-West Region**	(ex part of No 63 Group)
● **North-East Region**	(ex 64 Group)
● **Scotland & Northern Ireland Region**	(ex No 66 Group)

● **No 611 VGS**	Swanton Morley	Viking T1
● **No 612 VGS**	Benson	Vigilant T1
● **No 613 VGS**	Halton	Vigilant T1
● **No 614 VGS**	Wethersfield	Viking T1
● **No 615 VGS**	Kenley	Viking T1
● **No 616 VGS**	Henlow	Vigilant T1
● **No 617 VGS**	Manston	Viking T1
● **No 618 VGS**	West Malling	Viking T1
● **No 621 VGS**	Weston-s-Mare	Viking T1
● **No 622 VGS**	Upavon	Viking T1
● **No 624 VGS**	Chivenor	Vigilant T1
● **No 615 VGS**	South Cerney	Viking T1
● **No 626 VGS**	Predanack	Viking T1
● **No 631 VGS**	Sealand	Viking T1
● **No 632 VGS**	Ternhill	Vigilant T1
● **No 633 VGS**	Cosford	Vigilant T1
● **No 634 VGS**	St Athan	Viking T1
● **No 635 VGS**	Samlesbury	Vigilant T1
● **No 636 VGS**	Swansea	Viking T1
● **No 637 VGS**	Little Rissington	Viking T1
● **No 642 VGS**	Linton-on-Ouse	Vigilant T1
● **No 643 VGS**	Binbrook	Vigilant T1
● **No 644 VGS**	Syerston	Vigilant T1
● **No 645 VGS**	Catterick	Viking T1
● **No 661 VGS**	Kirknewton	Viking T1
● **No 662 VGS**	Arbroath	Viking T1
● **No 663 VGS**	Kinloss	Vigilant T1
● **ACCGS**	Syerston	Vigilant T1/Viking T1/Valiant T1/Janus C

Notes: No 643 VGS transferred from Scampton on 29 June 1991.

One further unit, No 664 VGS, temporarily stood-down in autumn 1990 following the closure of Bishop's Court, Northern Ireland.

An alternative site for Vigilants is being sought.

All units have devised unofficial badges, but none are applied to aircraft.

AIR EXPERIENCE FLIGHTS

Between two and six Chipmunks are assigned to each of 12 AEFs, the other having a single Bulldog. All were formed in October 1958. Some aircraft carry unofficial badges.

● No 1 AEF	Manston	Chipmunk T10	
● No 2 AEF	Hurn (Bournemouth)	Chipmunk T10	
● No 3 AEF	Filton	Chipmunk T10	
● No 4 AEF	Exeter	Chipmunk T10	
● No 5 AEF	Teversham (Cambridge)	Chipmunk T10	Badge: a winged 'V'
● No 6 AEF	Benson	Chipmunk T10	Badge: chalk hill horse
● No 7 AEF	Newton	Chipmunk T10	Badge: Robin Hood with a '7'
● No 8 AEF	Shawbury	Chipmunk T10	
● No 9 AEF	Finningley	Chipmunk T10	
● No 10 AEF	Woodvale	Chipmunk T10	Badge: a red rose
● No 11 AEF	Leeming	Chipmunk T10	Badge: a winged '11'
● No 12 AEF	Turnhouse (Edinburgh)	Chipmunk T10	
● No 13 AEF	Sydenham (Belfast Harbour)	Bulldog T1	

GROUND TRAINING UNITS

Limited space obviates a complete listing of non-flying units engaged in instruction. However, a number of these have static training airframes visible within their grounds or accessible at open days.

● **No 1 School of Technical Training**, Halton. Jaguar, Jet Provost, Harrier, Hunter, Gnat, Wessex and Whirlwind — approximately 107 airframes.

● **No 2 School of Technical Training**, Cosford. Jaguar, Jet Provost, Hunter, Harrier, Canberra, Buccaneer and others — approximately 45 airframes.

● **No 4 School of Technical Training**, St Athan. Jaguar, Jet Provost, Gnat and others — approximately 10 airframes.

● **Department of Special Ground Training**, Cranwell. Hunter — approximately 10 airframes.

● **Trade Management Training School**, Scampton. Hunter — approximately six airframes.

● **Battle Damage Repair Flight**, Abingdon. Buccaneer, Hunter, Canberra and others — approximately 12 aircraft (being dispersed).

Other significant instructional establishments are:

● **Bracknell** RAF Staff College
● **Hereford** Airmen's Command School
● **Henlow** Signals Engineering Establishment
● **Locking** No 1 Radio School
● **Newton** Guided Weapons School, School of Education, RAF Police School (including dog section)
● **Shawbury** Central Air Traffic Control School

MAINTENANCE UNITS

Air Officer Commanding Maintenance Units is responsible for Support Command bases repairing, overhauling and storing aircraft and equipment, as well as certain communications installations and some units lodging on Strike Command and RAF Germany stations. The main bases in this category which are wholly operated by Support Command are as below. Note that with the closure of Abingdon (Jaguar, Buccaneer and Hawk) and impending transfer of VC10 work from Brize Norton, St Athan is responsible for overhauling almost the entire RAF front line. Similar work on Support Command aircraft is allocated in some cases to private firms.

● **St Athan** Major aircraft overhaul facility. Includes Aircraft Engineering Wing (Nos 1, 2, 3, 4 and 10 Squadrons), General Engineering Wing (Nos 5, 6, 7 and 8 Squadrons) and Engineering Plans & Development Wing (No 9 Squadron) plus Repair & Salvage Squadron (from Abingdon 1992).

● Shawbury	Aircraft Storage Flight — approximately 60 aircraft
● Abingdon	Closed 31 July 1992.
● Cardington	No 217 MU (compressed gas production)
● Carlisle	No 14 MU (general storage)
● Chilmark	No 11 MU (ordnance store)
● Hartlebury	No 25 MU (general storage)
● Hullavington	Parachute Servicing Flight
● North Luffenham	Ground Radio Servicing Centre; Electronics Battle Damage Repair & Prevention Development Centre
● Quedgeley	No 7 MU (general and tri-service domestic equipment)
● Sealand	No 30 MU (avionics repair)
● Stafford	No 16 MU (general storage)
● Swanton Morley	Centralised Servicing Development Establishment

DIRECTLY ADMINISTERED UNITS

AOC Directly Administered Units is Strike Command's 'Lord High Everything Else', responsible for all units not falling into the categories of training or maintenance. These include hospitals at Halton, Wroughton, Ely (closing by March 1993) and Nocton Hall (reserve, administered by USAF Lakenheath); the much-maligned but excellent catering services; the RAF Institute of Aviation Medicine (IAM — formed 11 September 1950) and Battle of Britain Memorial Flight (BBMF — formed July 1957). The Balloon Operations Squadron at Hullavington will remain after the remainder of the base is closed, as will the Parachute Servicing Flight. A balloon detachment is based at Weston-on-the-Green for use by No 1 PTS at Abingdon. Several Signals Units (SUs) operate communications and radar installations. Support command also manages the RAF Mountain Rescue Service (formed 22 January 1944) with teams at Kinloss, Leuchars, Leeming, St Athan, Stafford and Valley.

● IAM	Farnborough	Hunter T7 (mod)/Jaguar T2A
● BBMF	Coningsby	Lancaster BI/Spitfire IIA/VB/PRXIX/Hurricane IIC/Devon C2/2/Chipmunk T10
● BOS	Hullavington	Kite Balloon D Mk IV and Mk XI MM

Non-flying:

● Digby	Nos 399 and 591 Signals Units
● Edelsborough	Communications site
● Lindholme	No 840 Signals Unit
● Oakhanger	No 1001 Signals Unit
● Rudloe Manor	No 6 Signals Unit; RAF Communications Centre
● Stanbridge	Joint Services Air Trooping Centre; Supply Control Centre
● Uxbridge	RAF Music Services

Non-flying, abroad:
● Akrotiri, Cyprus	No 280 Signals Unit
● Ayios Nikolaos, Cyprus	No 12 Signals Unit

RAF GLIDING AND SOARING ASSOCIATION

Formed on 15 December 1949, the RAFGSA is independent of the Ministry of Defence, although it does receive financial help from the RAF Sports Board and the Nuffield Trust, and is able to use military airfields for its weekend activities. Its aim is to 'bring gliding and soaring within the reach of all members of the RAF, with special regard to those employed on the ground'. Equipment is serialled in the range RAFGSA1 to RAFGSA99 with reuse of numbers when old aircraft are withdrawn. Powered tugs (eg, Chipmunks) are on the UK civil register. The following gliding clubs are based in the UK:

- RAFGSA Centre — Bicester
- Anglia GC — Wattisham
- Bannerdown GC — Hullavington
- Chilterns GC — Halton
- Clevelands GC — Dishforth
- Cranwell GC — Cranwell North
- Four Counties GC — Syerston
- Fenland GC — Marham
- Fulmar GC — Kinloss
- Humber GC — Scampton
- Wrekin GC — Cosford

Bases abroad with RAFGSA sailplanes are:
- Brüggen (Germany)
- Gütersloh (Germany)
- Kingsfield (Cyprus)
- Laarbruch (Germany)

Possibly unique in the RAF, in that it was granted by the College of Heralds two months before the unit formed, RAF Strike Command's badge combines the Astral Crown of the RAF with a sword from the badge of Fighter Command, lightning flashes from Bomber Command and a wavy annulet to suggest Coastal Command.

3 Aircraft and missiles

With the passage of time, aircraft are redesigned to adopt different roles, modified to take-on secondary tasks or rebuilt to do their work more efficiently. Such changes are normally accompanied by a variation of their mark number. With a few exceptions, aircraft receive a name in addition to the manufacturer's designation, the first variant of which is, logically enough, Mark 1. This is prefixed by letter or letters to indicate the aircraft's function, for example Tornado GR Mk 1 — usually written as GR1. A minor modification to the original GR (Ground attack and Reconnaissance) capability produces the GR1A, but a major redesign as an air superiority fighter yields the F2. With upgraded engines and avionics, this has become the F3, whilst the GR4 is shortly to appear through modification of GR1 airframes with the latest operational equipment.

Suffixes denote secondary roles or addition of special equipment. The Hercules C1(K) is a transport (C) having tanker (K) capability which either does not interfere with the primary role or can be easily removed. The Victor tanker is the K2 and not a B2(K) because the modifications prohibit the aircraft from dropping bombs and are, for all practical purposes, irreversible. Close study of designations will reveal numerous exceptions and inconsistencies, but the above is sufficient to outline the practice. Role prefixes and suffixes in current use are as below.

Prefixes:
- **AEW** Airborne Early Warning
- **C** Cargo (Transport)
- **D** Drone (formerly U - unmanned)
- **CC** Communications (ie VIP)
- **E** Electronic (calibration)
- **F** Fighter
- **FGR** Fighter Ground attack & Reconnaissance

- **GR** Ground attack & Reconnaissance
- **HAR** Helicopter, Air Rescue
- **HC** Helicopter, Cargo
- **HCC** Helicopter, Communications (ie VIP)
- **HT** Helicopter, Trainer
- **K** Tanker
- **KC** Tanker & Cargo (transport)
- **MR** Maritime Reconnaissance
- **PR** Photographic Reconnaissance
- **R** Reconnaissance (ELINT)
- **S** Strike (& attack)
- **T** Trainer
- **W** Weather (research)

Suffixes:
- **K** Tanker
- **P** Refuelling probe
- **PR** Photographic Reconnaissance

NOTES:

Some Hercules and Nimrods received (**P**) after their designation to denote addition of refuelling probes. Now that all aircraft of this type have been so modified, the differentiation is superfluous.

The designation Tornado GR1(T) and F3(T) for aircraft with dual control is occasionally seen, but is not official. All are fully combat-capable.

PRINCIPAL AIRCRAFT TYPES

This guide does not seek to duplicate basic specifications quoted in guides such as Ian Allan Ltd's *abc Combat Aircraft Recognition*. In the following pages, salient points are indicated for general interest or as a guide to further study.

Where applicable, manufacturers' names are those in use at the time at which the final aircraft was built.

Top:
● **British Aerospace Buccaneer S2B** Maritime strike/attack; Nos 12 and 208 Squadrons. 1 Ferranti ARI 5930 AIRPASS III ('Blue Parrot') radar; 2 No 12 Squadron badge; 3 BAe Sea Eagle anti-ship missile; 4 Rolls-Royce RB168 Spey turbofans (total two); 5 split tailcone opens outwards as an airbrake; 6 rear and front E-J band receiver for Marconi Sky Guardian radar warning receiver; 7 blown flaps (engine bleed air) for boundary layer control; 8 pitot probe: 9 C-D band receiver for Sky Guardian; 10 Westinghouse AN/ALQ-101(V)-10 jamming pod; 11 pilot and navigator under rear-sliding canopy; 12 fixed refuelling probe. Notes: A few S2A variants (lacking MARTEL and Sea Eagle capability) remain. Total 42 S2Bs received life-extension modifications 1986-90.

Above:
● **Boeing Helicopters Chinook HC1B** Medium-lift helicopter; Nos 7, 18 and 78 Squadrons and No 240 OCU. 1 Forward antenna for Marconi ARI 18228 radar warning receiver; 2 Nite Sun searchlight; 3 crew door (loadmaster observing lifting operation) and optional position for 7.62 mm machine-gun; 4 forward cargo hook (maximum 17,000lb); 5 main cargo hook (maximum 26,000lb); 6 rear cargo hook (maximum 17,000lb) — (total maximum load 26,000 lb); 7 chaff dispenser; 8 steerable rear wheel; 9 rear loading ramp; 10 flare dispenser; 11 rear antenna for ARI 18228; 12 No 78 Squadron badge; 13 Lycoming T55-L-712 turboshafts (total two); 14 two-man hoist; 15 pilot and co-pilot (cockpit optimised for night-vision goggles); Notes: Fleet being returned to Boeing for HC2 upgrade. Total 41 received; 33 remain.

Above:

● British Aerospace/McDonnell Douglas Harrier GR7 Short Take-Off/Vertical Landing (STO/VL) battlefield air interdiction and close air support; Nos 1, 3 and IV and 20 (Reserve) Squadrons, No 233 OCU and SAOEU. 1 Hughes Angle Rate Bombing Set (ARBS) sensor window; 2 GEC forward-looking infra-red (FLIR); 3 wind direction sensor (simple weathercock); 4 one-man cockpit (raised and modernised, compared with GR3); 5 Rolls-Royce Pegasus Mk 105 vectored-thrust turbofan; 6 front (cold) zero-scarf (non cut-away) nozzle; 7 inner wing pylon - max 2,000lb; 8 Sidewinder AAM pylon; 9 Marconi Zeus electronic countermeasures suite forward high-band receiver; 10 Zeus low-band receiver; 11 Zeus rear high-band receiver; 12 retracted outrigger wheel; 13 Plessey missile approach warning radar; 14 Zeus jamming transmitter; 15 Zeus low-band receiver; 16 rear (hot) jet nozzle; 17 ADEN 25 mm cannon pods; 18 centreline pylon - max 2,000lb; 19 outer wing pylon — max 620lb; 20 intermediate wing pylon — max 2,000lb (total permissible weapon load 13,235lb); 21 Zeus transmitters. Notes: GR5s (which have no FLIR bulge) being upgraded to GR7. Total 96 ordered; last 34 as GR7, others being upgraded. Further 13 two-seat Harrier T10s on order.

Below:

● British Aerospace Hawk T1A Advanced flying trainer (red/white/blue colours) and basic weapons trainer and target-tug (light grey); No 4 FTS, No 7 FTS CFS, Red Arrows, No 100 and Nos 19, 56, 74, 79 and 92 (Reserve) Squadrons. 1 Pitot tube; 2 ADEN 39 mm cannon pod; 3 BGT AIM-9L Sidewinder AAM; 4 No 63 Squadron 'checkerboard' (unit now disbanded); 5 Rolls-Royce/Turbomeca Adour Mk 151 turbofan; 6 raised rear cockpit for instructor; 7 single-piece canopy, hinged on starboard side; 8 Ferranti F195 gunsight. Notes: Items 2, 3 and 8 omitted on Hawk T1 flying trainers. Total 176 ordered; 89 converted to T1A; 150 remain.

Above:

● **Lockheed C-130K Hercules C1**
Tactical transport; Nos 24, 30, 47, and 70
Squadrons, No 1312 Flight and No 242
OCU. 1 Four-crew cockpit; 2 refuelling
probe; 3 Allison T55-A-15 turboprop
engines (total four); 4 rear loading ramp
(and aperture for refuelling hose of
tanker version); 5 1,132gall external fuel
tanks; 6 pannier for two mainwheels
each side; 7 position on Hercules C3 for
flat radome for station-keeping
equipment; 8 cargo hold for 64
paratroops or 42,670lb of freight (92 or
38,900lb in Hercules C3); 9 Ekco E290
radar. Notes: Hercules C1(K) is tanker
version; C3 fuselage 'stretched' by 15ft;
W2 is one-off research aircraft for DRA
Meteorological Research Flight. Total 66
bought; four lost.

Below:

● **SEPECAT Jaguar GR1A**
Attack and reconnaissance fighter; Nos
6, 41 and 54 and No 16 (Reserve)
Squadrons, No 226 OCU, SAOEU and
IAM. 1 Ferranti LRMTS (Laser Ranger
and Marked Target Seeker); 2 single-seat
cockpit; 3 No 6 Squadron unofficial
'winged can-opener' badge; 4 Marconi
ARI 18223 radar warning receiver; 5 No 6
Squadron's 'Gunners' Stripe' on RWR
pod; 6 rail for over-wing BGT AIM-9L
Sidewinder AAM; 7 Rolls-
Royce/Turbomeca Adour Mk 104
reheated turbofan (total two); 8 540lb
Mk2 bomb with parachute-retarding tail;
9 264gall drop-tanks; 10 ADEN 30mm
cannon; 11 pitot tube; 12 'Desert pink'
colour scheme; 13 low-viz European
green/grey wrap-round colour scheme.
Notes: T2A is two-seat trainer with
operational capability. Few unconverted
GR1/T2s extant. Total 165/38 built; 69/22
remain.

Above:

● **British Aerospace Nimrod MR2**
Maritime reconnaissance; Nos 120, 201 and 206 and No 38 (Reserve) Squadrons, No 236 OCU. ELINT; No 51 Squadron. 1 Thorn EMI ARI 5980 Searchwater radar; 2 weapons bay; 3 Rolls-Royce RB168-20 Spey turbofan (total four); 4 sonobuoy chutes; 5 rear-facing launcher for marker flares; 6 aerodynamic compensating fin for nose-probe; 7 MAD boom; 8 aerodynamic compensating fins for wingtip pods; 9 fin-tip 'banana' with satellite communications antenna; 10 Loral EW-1017 (ARI 18240/1) 'Yellow Gate' ESM pods; 11 searchlight (starboard side only); 12 eight or more tactical crew in cabin; 13 refuelling probe; 14 three flight-deck crew. Notes: Nimrod R1 has no MAD boom and additional aerials at several points. Total 48 MR1 and three R1 built; 33 MR2s and three R1s remain.

Below:

● **McDonnell Douglas F-4M Phantom FGR2**
Air defence fighter; Nos 56 and 74 Squadrons and No 1435 Flight. 1 Arms of the Falkland Islands; 2 SUU-23/A 20mm gun pod firing at up to 6,000 rounds/min; 3 BGT AIM-9L Sidewinder AAMs; 4 308gall drop-tank; 5 wing fold line; 6 two BAe Sky Flash AAMs under rear fuselage; 7 chaff and flare dispensers on rear of inner wing pylon; 8 Marconi ARI 18228 radar warning receiver; 9 No 1435 Flight unofficial marking; 10 Rolls-Royce Spey Mk202 reheated turbofan (total two); 11 navigator's cockpit; 12 pilot's cockpit (separate canopy); 13 Westinghouse AWG-12 radar. Notes: Phantom FG1 (ex Fleet Air Arm) withdrawn from service; last FGR2 squadron disbands October 1992. Total 52 FR1s, 118 FGR2s and 15 F-4J(UK)s acquired.

Above:

● **Westland/Aerospatiale SA330E Puma HC1**

Support helicopter; Nos 33 and 230 Squadrons, No 1563 Flight and No 240 OCU. 1 Forward antenna for Marconi ARI 18228 radar warning receiver; 2 'Polyvalent' air filters; 3 Turbomeca Turmo IIIC4 turboshaft (total two); 4 composites material rotor blade; 5 horizontal stabiliser (port only); 6 rear ARI 18228; 7 two Tracor M130 chaff/flare dispensers; 8 port rear sensor for Honeywell AN/AAR-47 missile plume detector; 9 retractable undercarriage; 10 sliding door to cabin and optional position for 7.62mm machine-gun; 11 cargo hook; 12 No 240 OCU badge; 13 forward port AN/AAR-47. Notes: Crew positions being changed to pilot, (added) navigator and loadmaster. Total 49 bought; 43 remain.

Below:

● **Westland/Sikorsky Sea King HAR3**

SAR helicopter; Nos 78 and 202 Squadrons and SKTF. 1 forward antenna for Marconi ARI 18228 radar warning receiver; 2 No 78 Squadron badge; 3 retractable undercarriage; 4 cargo hook; 5 sponson for buoyancy on water; 6 sliding cabin door; 7 boat hull; 8 rear ARI 18228; 9 break-line of folding tail; 10 MEL ARI 5955 radar; 11 two-man winch; 12 Rolls-Royce Gnome H1400-1 turboshaft (total two); 13 two pilots (radar operator and winchman in cabin). Notes: No 202 Squadron aircraft lack ARI 18228. Total 19 built; six more on order.

Below:

● **Boeing E-3D Sentry AEW1**
Airborne early warning; No 8 Squadron and STS. 1 Bendix-King weather radar; 2 four flight-deck crew; 3 exhaust for auxiliary power unit; 4 HF radio antenna on wing trailing edge; 5 Loral EW-1017 (ARI 18240/1) 'Yellow Gate' ESM pod; 6 Westinghouse AN/APY-2 radar rotodome; 7 CFM International CFM56-2A turbofan (total four); 8 13-person tactical crew; 9 No 8 Squadron 'fighter bars' astride roundel; 10 receptacle for USAF-style 'flying boom' refuelling; 11 probe for RAF-style drogue refuelling. Notes: Wingtip pods only on RAF E-3s. Total seven aircraft.

Bottom:

● **Panavia Tornado GR1/1A**
Strike/attack and (GR1A) reconnaissance; Nos II, IX, 13, 14, 17, 27, 31 and 617 and No XV (Reserve) Squadrons, TTTE, TWCU and SAOEU. 1 Texas Instruments radar and terrain-following radar; 2 pilot; 3 navigator (some aircraft have minimal-standard dual control added); 4 port forward antenna for Marconi Hermes radar homing and warning receiver; 5 Turbo Union RB199 Mk 103 reheated turbofans (total two); 6 rear Hermes antenna; 7 Marconi Sky Shadow jamming pod (Bofors BOZ 103 chaff/flare pod on starboard side); 8 495gall drop-tank (reduces maximum wing-sweep from 67° to 63°); 9 BGT AIM-9L Sidewinder self-defence AAM; 10 Ferranti TIALD laser-designator pod (or up to eight 1,000lb bombs); 11 position for under-fuselage sensor on GR1A; 12 Gulf War 'nose art' (and position of side window — port and starboard — on GR1A); 13 Ferranti LRMTS (Laser-Ranger and Marked Target Seeker); 14 IWKA-Mauser 27mm cannon (total two). Notes: GR1s to be converted to GR4 standard. Total 219 production aircraft; 36 lost.

Above:

● **Panavia Tornado F3**
Air defence; Nos 11, 23, 25, 29, 43 and 111 and No 65 (Reserve) Squadrons, No 229 OCU and F3OEU. 1 Marconi AI 24 'Foxhunter' radar; 2 BAe Sky Flash AAMs; 3 variable geometry wings, sweeping between 25° and 67°; 4 Turbo Union RB199 Mk104 reheated turbofans; 5 all-moving stabilator; 6 extended reheat pipe of Mk104 engine; 7 leading-edge slats extended for improved low-speed handling; 8 BGT AIM-9L Sidewinder AAM (optionally, second on outer side of pylon); 9 badge of No 229 OCU; 10 pilot and navigator. Notes: Tornado F2 in storage, apart from trials use; may be converted to F2A (with F3's avionics upgrades). Total 171 production aircraft; one lost.

Above:

● **Lockheed 1011 TriStar K1**
Tanker, (KC1) tanker-transport and (C2) passenger transport; No 216 Squadron and No 241 OCU. 1 Refuelling probe (removed from KC1; not fitted to C2); 2 four flight deck crew; 3 cabin freight space forward and 187 seats at rear (up to 266 seats or all freight in KC1; 267 seats in C2); 4 Rolls-Royce RB211-524B turbofan (two under wings); 5 air duct for third RB211; 6 No 216 Squadron badge; 7 flaps extended for landing; 8 two FRL Mk17T hose-and-drum units; 9 four-wheel main undercarriage bogies; 10 under-floor tanks for extra 12,830gall of fuel, increasing total to 38,885gall. Notes: C2s have normal tankage and to be upgraded to C2A with K1/KC1's military avionics. Total two K1s, four KC1s and three C2s.

Below:

● **BAC VC10 K2**
Tanker and C1(K) tanker-transport; Nos 10 and 101 Squadron and No 241 OCU. 1 Four-man flight-deck; 2 forward cabin for 17 passengers, remainder occupied by extra tanks for 3,500gall of fuel, total capacity 20,737gall (22,609gall in K3); 3 badge of No 101 Squadron; 4 fore and aft antennae for Marconi Sky Guardian radar warning receiver in fin 'bullet'; 5 exhaust for auxiliary power unit; 6 drogue of starboard hose; 7 FRL Mk17B hose-and-drum unit; 8 Rolls-Royce Conway turbofan (total four); 9 closed-circuit TV camera; 10 FRL Mk32/2800 wing pod; 11 fuel receiver probe. Notes: Total five K2s and four K3s; all remain. Under conversion are 13 VC10 C1s of No 10 Squadron to C1(K) with two Mk32 HDUs only; and five ex-airline Super VC10s to K4 with one Mk17 and two Mk32s. Neither conversion involves extra tankage.

Above:
● **Handley-Page Victor K2**
Tanker; No 55 Squadron. 1 Visual bomb-aiming windows remaining from aircraft's time as a B2; 2 H2S Mk9 ground-mapping radar; 3 slipper tanks — 1,745gall each; 4 FRL Mk20B refuelling pod; 5 Marconi ARI 18228 radar warning receiver fore and aft in fin 'bullet'; 6 No 55 Squadron badge; 7 ram air turbine emergency air scoops extended; 8 fuel tanks in bomb bay, totalling 4,615gall; 9 Rolls-Royce Conway Mk201 turbofan (total four); 10 fuel receiver probe; 11 four-man cockpit; 12 housing for terrain-avoidance radar (removed). Notes: total fuel capacity of 16,385gall exceeds permitted 238,000lb maximum take-off weight by about 750gall. Total 22 conversions; being progressively withdrawn.

Below:
● **Westland Wessex HC5C**
Support and SAR helicopter (HC2 and HC5C); Nos 22, 28, 72 and 84 Squadrons, No 2 FTS, Queen's Flight and SARTS. 1 Starboard front Honeywell AN/AAR-47 missile approach warning receiver; 2 engine exhaust; 3 emergency flotation bag stowage; 4 cabin with first aid equipment and stretcher; 5 sliding door; 6 light blue United Nations band (No 84 Squadron only); 7 starboard rear AN/AAR-47; 8 aircraft identification symbol within No 84 Squadron; 9 two-man hoist (300ft); 10 two-seat cockpit. Notes: UK-based SAR HC2s are yellow; all-red HCC4s operated by The Queen's Flight. Total 72 HC2s; two HCC4s, six ex-Navy HC5Cs; 61/2/5 respectively remain.

SECONDARY AIRCRAFT TYPES

Below:

● **BAe 780 Andover E3**
Calibration and (C1) transport; Nos 32 and 115 Squadrons and ATF. 1 Milligan Lamp (omitted from C1 and E3A); 2 'kneeling' main undercarriage for easier rear loading; 3 rear loading ramp; 4 red fin, central fuselage and engine nacelles on E3/E3A; 5 Litton (Canada) Inc Inertially-Referenced Flight Inspection System for calibration (not in C1 and E3A); 6 two-man cockpit; 7 No 115 Squadron badge. Notes: passenger transport C1s of No 32 Squadron have no red in colour scheme. Total 31 C1s

built; six C1s, two C1(PR)s, four E3s and two E3As remain; C1(PR) has under-fuselage cameras and sealed forward freight door (port).

Bottom:

● **BAe 748 Andover CC2**
Communications; No 32 Squadron and ATF. 1 Rolls-Royce Dart Mk201 (total two); 2 passenger cabin; 3 'straight' fuselage of civilian BAe 748; 4 rear passenger door; 5 forward freight door. Notes: Three of six aircraft built are ex-Queen's Flight.

Above:
● **BAe 125 Dominie T1**
Navigation trainer; No 6 FTS. 1 Ekco E190 radar; 2 twin mainwheel undercarriage; 3 flaps fully extended for landing; 4 Rolls-Royce Viper 301 turbojet (total two); 5 two students and one instructor in cabin; 6 dual control cockpit. Notes: All Dominies have a red and white colour scheme.

Below:
● **BAe 146 CC2**
VVIP communications; The Queen's Flight and No 241 OCU. 1 Two-crew flight deck; 2 VVIP interior; 3 Lycoming ALF 504R-5 turbofan (total four); 4 'petal' airbrakes form rear fuselage; 5 Northrop MIRTS infra-red jammers in pods; 6 rear passenger door. Total two C1 and three C2 acquired; three C2s remain.

Top:
● **British Aerospace Bulldog T1**
Primary trainer; No 1 FTS, UASs (16), No
13 AEF, CFS. 1 Fixed undercarriage; 2
East Midlands UAS badge; 3 rearwards-
sliding hood to dual control cockpit; 4
Textron Lycoming IO-360-A1B6 piston
engine. Total 130 bought; 118 remain.

Above:
● **De Havilland DHC-1 Chipmunk T10**
Air experience/grading trainer; AEFs
(12), CFS, EFTS, Berlin Station Flight. 1
DH Gipsy Major 8 piston engine with
cartridge starter; 2 fixed undercarriage; 3
tailwheel - unique in 'non-historic' RAF
aircraft; 4 No 6 AEF badge; 5 rear-sliding
canopy; 6 high-visibility black and white
propeller stripes. Total 740 acquired; 75
remain.

Above:
● **BAC Canberra T17A**
Electronic countermeasures training; No 360 Squadron and (T4) CTF. 1 I-band transmitting and receiving antennae around nose cone; 2 D-band blade aerial; 3 bomb bay containing 2,000lb of electrical equipment with air scoops for cooling; 4 air scoop cooling turbo-generators installed to produce additional electrical power; 5 blade aerial for GTE Dragonfly surveillance and jamming equipment (not fitted to T17); 6 provision for wing-tip tanks modified to distribute 'chaff'; 7 rear I-band antennae; 8 No 360 Squadron markings; 9 Rolls-Royce Avon Mk101 turbojet (total two); 10 terminal for HF wire aerial to fin-top. Notes: Canberra T4 has two seats beneath canopy; B2 has transparent nose. Total 24 T17 conversions, of which six to T17A; numbers diminishing.

Below:
● **BAe Harrier T4**
Combat-capable trainer for Harrier GR5/7; No 20 (Reserve) Squadron, No 1417 Flight, No 233 OCU and Gütersloh SF. 1 Front cockpit; 2 raised rear cockpit with dual controls; 3 scarfed front (cold air) movable nozzles; 4 Rolls-Royce Pegasus Mk103 vectored-thrust turbofan; 5 metal wing, smaller than GR5/7's carbon fibre unit; 6 forward antenna for Marconi ARI 18223 radar warning receiver; 7 extended tail cone with rear ARI 18223 antenna at tip; 8 outrigger wheels close to wing-tip; 9 MATRA 155 launch pod for nineteen 68mm SNEB rockets; 10 100gall drop-tank; 11 ADEN 30mm canon pod (total two); 12 CBLS 100 practice-bomb carrier; 13 badge of No 233 OCU; 14 Ferranti LRMTS (Laser-Ranger and Marked Target Seeker). Notes: Fitment of pointed nose as replacement for LRMTS changes mark to T4A. Harrier GR3 is single-seat version with No 1417 Flight and partly equipping OCU. Total 118 GR1/1A/3 and 28 T2/2A/4/4A built.

Above:

● **Hawker-Siddeley Hunter T7**
Two-seat advanced trainer (T7/T7A/T8B);
Nos 12 and 208 Squadrons and IAM. 1
Badge of No 12 Squadron; 2 ADEN 30
mm cannon (starboard only); 3 100gall
drop-tank; 4 optional pylon with 100gall
drop-tank; 5 ventral airbrake; 6 optional
arrestor hook; 7 Rolls-Royce Avon
Mk115 turbojet; 8 optional ILS whip
aerial; 9 fairing for outboard pylon
explosive jettison cartridge; 10 optional
IFIS (Integrated Flight Instrumentation
System) for port-side pilot (resembling
Buccaneer instrumentation); 11 optional
ADD (Airflow Detection Device — as in
Buccaneer) sensor on port side of
forward fuselage. Notes: Numerous
permutations of above-mentioned
optional equipment on Mks 7 and 8 for
Buccaneer pilot training.

Below:

● **Westland/Aerospatiale SA 341D
Gazelle HT3**
Training and communications helicopter;
No 32 Squadron, No 2 FTS and CFS. 1
dual control with bench seat for three at
rear; 2 Turbomeca Astazou III turboshaft
engine; 3 transmission to tail rotor; 4
'Fenestron' (or 'fan-in-fin') tail rotor; 5
fixed skid landing gear. Total 30 built; 27
remain, plus four Navy HT2s on loan.

Top:
● **Hunting Jet Provost T5A**
Basic (navigation) trainer; Nos 1, 6 and 7 FTSs and CFS. 1 anti-spin strakes (not on No 6 FTS aircraft); 2 attachment for optional 48gall wingtip fuel tanks (No 6 FTS only; tank fitment allows anti-spin strake removal); 3 'CF' logo of Church Fenton-based No 7 FTS (aircraft of Refresher Flying Flight); 4 Type A roundel; 5 dual control, pressurised cockpit; 6 anti-glare panel; 7 glide slope aerial (handle-shaped) indicates conversion from Mk5 to 5A. Notes: Being withdrawn from service following Jet Provost T3A (different canopy design). Some unconverted T5s remain with No 6 FTS. Total 200 T3s and 110 T5s built.

Above:
● **BAe 201 Jetstream T1**
Twin-conversion and aircrew trainer; No 6 FTS. 1 Dual control cockpit; 2 cabin with four passenger seats; 3 Turbomeca Astazou XVID turboprop (total two). Notes: 26 acquired; 11 remain.

Below:
● **Shorts S312 Tucano T1**
Basic trainer; Nos 1 and 3 FTSs, and CFS. 1 Garrett TPE331-12B turboshaft engine; 2 two-piece canopy covering student and (in raised rear cockpit) instructor; 3 airbrake in extended position; 4 twin exhausts add 51hp in equivalent thrust. Notes: Aircraft destined for No 6 FTS will have staff pilot in front cockpit and student navigator in rear. Total 130 procured.

Above:
● **BAC VC10 C1**
Strategic transport; No 101 Squadron and No 241 OCU. 1 Optional podded infra-red jammer: Loral Matador (three rectangular windows) or Lockheed-Sanders Yukon Jack (single circular window); 2 No 10 Squadron badge; 3 Rolls-Royce Conway Mk 301 (total four); 4 cabin for up to 150 passengers in rear-facing seats; 5 four-crew cockpit; 6 refuelling probe. Notes: Total 14 bought; 13 remain — all being converted to tanker capability.

Below:
● **Grob 109B Vigilant T1**
Power-assisted (self-launching) sailplane; Nos 612, 613, 616, 624, 632, 633, 635, 637, 642, 643, 644 and 663 VGSs, ACCGS and CFS. 1 Two-seat, side-by-side cockpit; 2 glass fibre construction; 3 fixed and spatted undercarriage; 4 downwards view window; 5 75hp Limbach piston engine. Notes: 53 bought.

Bottom:
● **Grob 103 Viking T1**
Sailplane; Nos 611, 614, 615, 617, 618, 621, 622, 625, 626, 627, 636, 645, 661 and 662 VGSs, ACCGS and CFS. 1 Auxiliary nosewheel; 2 mainwheel; 3 auxiliary tailwheel; 4 skids on wingtips; 5 T-tail; 6 wing spoilers extended for landing; 7 two-sear, tandem cockpit; 8 attachment for towing cable. Notes: Winch-launched. Total 100 bought; 94 remain.

OTHER RAF AIRCRAFT

Above:
● Pilatus/Britten-Norman Islander CC2
One aircraft for No 32 Squadron. (Army
Islander illustrated)

Below.
● De Havilland Devon C2/2
One aircraft with Battle of Britain
Memorial Flight

Above:
● Schleicher ASW-19 Valiant T1
Four aircraft with ACCGS.

Above:
● Schempp-Hirth Janus C
Two aircraft with ACCGS.

HISTORIC RAF AIRCRAFT

Above:
● Hawker Hurricane IIC
Battle of Britain Memorial Flight.

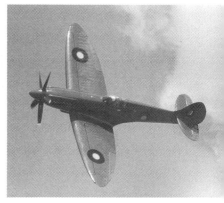

Above:
● Supermarine 390 Spitfire PRXIX
Battle of Britain Memorial Flight.

Above:
● Avro 683 Lancaster B1
Battle of Britain Memorial Flight.

Below:
● Avro 698 Vulcan B2: Vulcan Display
Flight

RAF AIRCRAFT IN MOD(PE) SERVICE

Following their withdrawal from RAF service, the aircraft illustrated have been transferred to the Ministry of Defence (Procurement Executive) for trials work:

Above:
● BEAGLE 206 Basset CC1
Empire Test Pilots' School - variable stability.

Below:
● North American/Noorduyn Harvard IIB
Aeroplane & Armament Experimental Establishment - photography.

Above:
● BAC P26 Lightning F6
British Aerospace — Tornado radar
trials.

Below:
● Gloster Meteor D16
Defence Research Agency (Aerospace
Division) — unmanned target tug.

Bottom:
● Vickers 668 Varsity T1, Defence
Research Agency (Aerospace Division)
— night vision systems. DRA also
operates directly procured aircraft
including the Douglas C-47, Piper
Chieftain, DH Comet, BAC 1-11 and BAC
Viscount.

RAF AIR-LAUNCHED MISSILES

Above:
● British Aerospace ALARM
'Air-Launched Anti-Radar Missile'.
Carried by Tornado GR1.

Above:
● Hawker-Siddeley/MATRA AS37
MARTEL
'Missile Anti-Radar/TELevision'. Carried
by Buccaneer S2B (anti-radar version
only).

Above:
● BAe Sea Eagle
Sea-skimming anti-ship missile. Carried
by Buccaneer S2B (to be fitted to
Tornado GR1 from 1993).

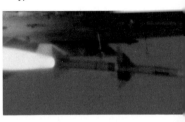

Above:
● BAe Sky Flash
Semi-active radar homing AAM. Carried
by Tornado F3 and Phantom FGR2.
(Same shape as Sparrow)

Above:
● Raytheon AIM-7E2 Sparrow
Semi-active radar-homing AAM. In
reserve for Sky Flash.

Above:
● Bodenseewerk Gerätetechnik AIM-9L
Sidewinder
Infra red-homing AAM. Carried
offensively by Tornado F3, Phantom
FGR2 and Hawk T1A; for self-defence by
Buccaneer S2B, Harrier GR3/GR5/GR7,
Jaguar GR1A and Tornado GR1/GR1A;
applicable to Nimrod MR2.

Identification is of great importance in the military world. Aircraft of the RAF are always marked with the internationally recognised national colours of the United Kingdom and a serial number; optionally they may wear the badge of their operating unit, an individual letter or number assigned by that operator and other special markings.

NATIONAL MARKINGS

International convention requires military aircraft to signify their country of origin in a recognised manner. The UK applies a circular device which, on non-combatant aircraft, includes the national colours of red (in the centre), white and blue. This is generally described as a 'roundel', although 'cockade' (normally associated with the French, in whose markings the order of the colours is reversed) is more correct. In heraldry, a roundel is a disc of one colour, so the UK's marking is actually three roundels of different size, superimposed.

The usual style of non-tactical roundel presentation is currently Type 'D', in which the colours are symmetrical: if 'd' is the diameter of the whole (ie, blue), then white

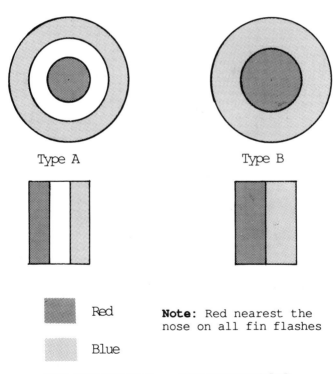

Type A   Type B

Red

Blue

Note: Red nearest the nose on all fin flashes

NATIONAL MARKINGS

Above:
Most RAF aircraft are serialled in the XA-XZ and ZA-ZH ranges. The F-series code on this helicopter identifies it as a Puma of No 240 OCU. *Paul Jackson*

Below:
Instructional serials are suffixed M, as on these Jet Provosts at No 1 SoTT, Halton. 8962M (nearest) was formerly XM371. Blue crosses indicate the aircraft do not come within the scope of the Conventional Forces in Europe equipment count. *Paul Jackson*

is two-thirds 'd' and red is one-third 'd'. Tactical aircraft omit the white because this high-visibility colour would compromise their camouflage. Such roundels are termed Type 'B' but, again, that is not wholly correct. The original Type 'B' of World War 2 had the red centre of two-fifths of diameter, whereas in the modern version it is one-half. Aircraft of the RAF (but not the Fleet Air Arm or Army Air Corps) have a square or rectangular (but occasionally raked-back) fin flash equally proportioned red/white/blue or red/blue to correspond with the roundel. It should be noted that fin flashes are 'handed' so that the red is nearest the nose on both sides. Aircraft wearing light coloured camouflage will have pale red and blue in their roundels and flashes.

MILITARY SERIALS

A complete listing of current UK military aircraft and an explanation of their serial number systems appears in *abc Military Aircraft Markings*, published annually by Ian Allan Ltd. It must therefore suffice here to give only a brief outline of the numbering found on RAF aircraft.

There is a unified system for all UK military aircraft which is now drawing to the end of the two-letters-plus-three-digits range introduced in 1940. Most serving RAF aircraft are in the batches XA100-XZ999 and ZA101-ZZ999, current allocations having reached the late ZH range. In addition to omitting letters C, I, O, Q, U and Y, (so ZJ will follow ZH) batches of numbers are left blank at random — the so-called 'blackout blocks'. Blackouts appear between serial ranges for different aircraft types and within individual ranges. For example:

- ZD990-ZD993   Harrier T4
- ZD996-ZD998   Tornado GR1
- ZE114-ZE126   Tornado GR1
- ZE144-ZE147   Tornado GR1
- ZE154-ZE168   Tornado F3

The purpose of blackouts was to make it difficult to assess the number of aircraft built from the evidence of a few serial numbers. Official inertia perpetuates the practice, even though the MoD and manufacturers now publish the quantities of most aircraft procured.

Aircraft grounded for instructional purposes are normally assigned a new serial (though many do not wear it) suffixed 'M'. This series, which has no blackouts, has recently passed 9100M.

CODES

Within an individual unit, an aircraft's full serial number is generally only of interest to those responsible for compiling maintenance records. For most other purposes, a single letter or number will suffice as an 'in house' identity. As most combat squadrons have 12 aircraft, the letters of the alphabet are adequate and generally used. Training units with over 26 machines often adopt fleet numbers or sometimes the 'last-three' of the serial.

Whilst the above-mentioned systems usually begin at 'A' and '1' (or '01'), there are exceptions. If two squadrons are sharing the same station, they may take different halves of the alphabet. Extending this farther, almost the entire fleets of certain tactical aircraft have two-letter codes, the first of which identifies the operator. Because of equipment exchanges between squadrons, such two-letter codes are not permanently wedded to a serial number. Tornado GR1 codes were allocated in batches to RAF Germany operating bases in squadron number order, whereas Tornado F3 codes were assigned alphabetically in chronological order of squadron conversion to the type.

Tornado GR1:
- AA-AZ   No IX Squadron, Brüggen
- BA-BZ   No 14 Squadron, Brüggen
- CA-CZ   No 17 Squadron, Brüggen
- DA-DZ   No 31 Squadron, Brüggen
- EA-EZ   No XV Squadron, Laarbruch
- FA-FZ   No 16 Squadron, Laarbruch
- GA-GZ   No 20 Squadron, Laarbruch
- HA-HZ   reserved (for No 2 Squadron?)
- JA-JZ   No 27 Squadron, Marham
- KA-KZ   reserved (for No 13 Squadron?)
- LA-LZ   reserved (for No 45 Squadron?)
- MA-MZ   No 617 Squadron, Marham
- TA-TZ   TWCU, Honington

(The Laarbruch Wing has disbanded)

Tornado F3:
- AA-AZ   No 229 OCU, Coningsby
- A1-A9   No 229 OCU 'overflow' 1991
- BA-BZ   No 29 Squadron, Coningsby
- CA-CZ   No 5 Squadron, Coningsby
- DA-DZ   No 11 Squadron, Leeming
- EA-EZ   No 23 Squadron, Leeming
- FA-FZ   No 25 Squadron, Leeming
- GA-GZ   No 43 Squadron, Leuchars
- HA-HZ   No 111 Squadron, Leuchars

Jaguar GR1A:
- EA-EZ   No 6 Squadron, Coltishall
- FA-FZ   No 41 Squadron, Coltishall

● GA-GZ   No 54 Squadron, Coltishall
(AA-DZ previously used by Nos 14, 17, 20 and 31 Squadrons before receiving Tornados)

Harrier GR7:
● AA-AZ   No 3 Squadron, Gütersloh
● CA-CZ   No IV Squadron, Gütersloh

Support helicopters:
● BA-BZ   No 18 Squadron (Chinook)
● CA-CZ   No 33 Squadron (Puma)
● DA-DZ   No 230 Squadron (Puma)
● EA-EZ   No 7 Squadron (Chinook)
● FA-FZ   No 240 OCU (both)

Canberra:
● AA-AZ   No 1 PRU
● BA-BZ   No 231 OCU
● CA-CZ   No 100 Squadron
● EA-EZ   No 360 Squadron
(No 100 retains its codes despite conversion to Hawks)

Squadrons assigned a trainer version of their front-line type will usually apply the code 'T'. Additional trainers may use 'X-Z'. More inventive units select letters to allow their aircraft to spell names for example 'SHINY TWO II AC' (AC = Army Co-operation) for No II Squadron and 'TIGER SQN' for No 74. A few University Air Squadrons have caught the bug, such as 'C-U-A-S' and 'L-U-A-S' at Cambridge and Liverpool respectively, as has No 8 Air Experience Flight: '8-A-E-F'. More subtle still are the different coloured propeller spinners used by Glasgow & Strathclyde UAS and Queens UAS; and No 84 Squadron's unique system of identifying its five Wessex by playing card symbols: heart, club, spade, diamond and joker.

BADGES

The badges assigned to RAF units are frequently and incorrectly described as 'crests' or even 'coats of arms'. The only proper name is badge, and many badges have an interesting origin which repays study. Badges must be approved by the College of Arms, the current Inspector of RAF Badges being the Surrey Herald of Arms, and comprise a subject surrounded by a wreath of leaves, surmounted by a crown and with a motto in a scroll beneath. The original grant is signed by the monarch of the day and the Inspector, the first such approvals taking place in May 1936.

Rarely is the full badge applied to an aircraft, normal procedure being to display the subject — such as the Greek 'pi' and Maltese cross of No 22 Squadron (Malta because the squadron was based there when it applied for a badge; 'pi' because as part of No 7 Wing in World War 1 it had '22/7' on a board above its HQ's entrance — and $\frac{22}{7}$ equals 'pi in arithmetic'). A very few units use an unauthorised device to proclaim their identity: No 6 Squadron's badge is an eagle preying on a serpent, but its aircraft are marked with a winged can-opener to recall its tank-busting success in World War 2. No 12 Squadron appears to conform with its official fox's mask (face), yet close inspection reveals that on each aircraft it is slightly different.

In the case of a subject which has a recognisable front and back (ie, it faces in one direction — invariably to the left on the badge), that representation will be applied to the port (left) side of the aircraft. A mirror image is painted on the starboard, so that — for example   in the case of No 11 Squadron's two eagles, they are not seen to be flying backwards at Mach 2 on the right side of Tornado F3s.

The only RAF flying unit to have a grant of arms (rather than a badge) and apply it in full to its aircraft is the Central Flying School. It is therefore correct to refer to CFS aircraft carrying the unit's arms (or coat of arms). UAS Bulldogs are often marked with

Left:
A rare case of arms being applied to an aircraft (in this instance a Jaguar T2). Very different in appearance to a badge, the coat of arms of the Empire Test Pilots' School. *Paul Jackson*

Below:
One of the best known fighter-badges is the tiger's face of No 74 Squadron. The tiger-striped 'fighter bars' formerly flanked the fuselage roundel. *Paul Jackson*

Bottom:
University Air Squadrons are part of the RAF Volunteer Reserve and their badges reflect the arms of the university(ies) they serve. *Paul Jackson*

part of their University's arms, but in the form of an approved badge. Outside the RAF, the A&AEE has arms, of which part are displayed in the form of an unapproved badge, as does the ETPS. Aircraft of the Defence Research Agency (Aerospace Division) may still be seen wearing the old Royal Aerospace Establishment arms.

OTHER MARKINGS

Camouflage is the most obvious additional marking to be found on tactical aircraft. Low-level operators use dark green and dark sea grey, and if the undersides of their aircraft are similarly painted, they are said to have 'wrap-around' camouflage. Addition to this of black serials and titles, plus Type 'B' roundels produces a 'low-viz' (low visibility) colour scheme. Air defence fighters use medium-level camouflage of three light greys: medium sea grey, mixed grey (known as Barley grey after its deviser, Phil Barley); and light aircraft grey. Large aircraft (VC10 K2/K3, Nimrod and Victor) wear a colour known as hemp which is to afford obscurity when parked on toned-down concrete. Medium Grey has recently become popular with BAe 125s, Wessex and Buccaneers. For the Gulf War, a sandy-pink washable paint was applied to several types of aircraft and invariably became known as 'Pink Panther' or 'Desert Pink'. In correct nomenclature 'washable' is ARTF Alkali-Removable Temporary Finishing.

Insignia of rank will be seen on the cockpit sides of some aircraft. Since the 1960s, officer's ranks have been out of step with their responsibilities due to a general upgrading. Group Captains captain wings; Wing Commanders command squadrons; and Squadron Leaders lead flights. A 12-aircraft squadron is usually divided into 'A' and 'B' Flights, each run by an officer of Squadron Leader rank, who will paint a rectangular flag ('air force blue' with red and royal blue horizontal stripes) on his aircraft. The squadron's commander will apply a Wing Commander's triangular pennant, containing two thin red stripes — or, in the rare, but unknown, case of a squadron being led by a Group Captain, a pennant with one broad red stripe.

Finally — and hardly liable to be missed — are the special colour schemes applied for anniversaries. A rash of 75th anniver-

saries for squadrons has recently passed, but 1993 marks the 75th birthday of the RAF and the 25th of Strike Command, for which appropriate adornments will doubtless be devised.

RADIO IDENTITIES

Callsigns used by military aircraft rarely are related to their serial number and will usually change after every flight. Several systems are in use by the RAF, of which the most common is the tri-graph of three letters or a number and two letters (followed by two numbers to indicate the individual aircraft). Whilst this system can, and does, use any combination at random, training units tend to use a permanent tri-graph closely related to the name of their base. Examples are:

- CHV   No 7 FTS, Chivenor
- COT   TTTE, Cottesmore
- CWL   No 3 FTS, Cranwell
- FYT   No 6 FTS, Finningley
- FYY   No 6 FTS, Finningley
- LON   No 1 FTS, Linton-on-Ouse
- LOP   No 1 FTS, Linton-on-Ouse
- LOS   No 226 OCU, Lossiemouth
- TOF   RNEFTS, Topcliffe
- SAP   CFS, Scampton
- SWD   EFTS, Swinderby
- SYS   No 2 FTS, Shawbury
- VYT   No 4 FTS, Valley

Transports use a four-figure number prefixed 'Ascot' or 'RRR' and tactical squadrons use either a tri-graph or a word and number, such as 'Snake' for No 14 Squadron, 'Fresco' for No 23 and 'Trent' for No 27. No 72 Squadron has been heard using 'Swift' which is, of course, the subject of the squadron badge.

Some words have become well known as call-signs, perhaps the most widely-recognised being 'Kitty' for The Queen's Flight, which also uses 'Rainbow' when lesser mortals are aboard. Others include:

- 'Blackbox'   DRA
- 'Gauntlet'   Boscombe Down (A&AEE, ETPS, SAOEU)
- 'Nugget'   DRA
- 'Magic'   all E-3 Sentries
- 'Tester'   ETPS

The list is endless... but that is the reason for call-signs.

Whilst the ultimate purpose of the armed services is to fight in defence of their country and its interests, it would be more correct to say that their first duty was deterrence. In four and a half decades of uneasy peace between the end of World War 2 and the collapse of the Warsaw Pact, the role of the RAF, the other two UK armed services and their NATO allies was to define the borders of the 'Free West' and make clear the ability and determination to resist aggression. In providing an air defence fighter force and a fleet of nuclear-armed bombers, the RAF played a vital role during what became known as the Cold War. This undeclared conflict may be seen to have ended with the self-destruction of communism and the Soviet Union that was its first home.

Even before peace had completely broken out in Europe, the RAF was involved in a new conflict. The Iraqi invasion of Kuwait and the United Nations' offensive in January-February 1991 to eject Iraqi forces from occupied territory may be indicative of new directions in which the armed forces of democracy must face. A year after the Gulf War, a small contingent of RAF reconnaissance Jaguars was keeping watch over the UN-protected area of northern Iraq in which the Kurdish people are in danger from their tyrannical ruler in Baghdad. Such operations by Western forces are likely to increase as large states break up into quarrelsome republics and Third World dictators develop their own chemical and nuclear weapons and delivery systems.

Publication of this book finds the RAF in the process of contracting as a result of the collapse of the Warsaw Pact, but still not fully sure of the fresh challenges which await it in the 'New World Order'. The one certainty is that preparedness for the usually sudden onset of conflict is only assured by regular and rigorous training in peacetime. For the foreseeable future, therefore, the RAF will continue to police the UK's skies and maintain its aircrew at the peak of training by the frequent exercise of its undoubted skills.

QUICK REACTION ALERT (Interceptor)

Invariably abbreviated to 'Q', this represents the first line of air defence for the UK.

Although foreign aircraft may fly within three miles of the coast without infringing British sovereignty, they will have long before have appeared on NATO radar screens. Civil and military aircraft which have filed a flight plan may proceed at will; those which have not may find themselves with a free escort service provided by the RAF.

Whilst NATO is a skeletal organisation in peacetime (that is to say, its earmarked forces are under national control until the transition to war) there is one exception in the form of the air defence force. Here, all members exchange information, so that, for example, if a long-range maritime reconnaissance aircraft takes off from northern Russia and passes westwards through Norwegian airspace, the RAF will be aware of its movements well before it arrives at the borders of the UK Air Defence Region (UKADR) or comes within range of the radar site on the Faroe Islands (see chapter 7).

There are two principal categories of CIS tourist: maritime reconnaissance aircraft (usually the Tupolev Tu-142 Bear) flying north of Scotland to reach the Atlantic and electronic intelligence aircraft (often Tupolev Tu-16 Badgers) investigating the East Coast radar defences. Numbers of both have fallen in recent years, such that the QRA effort has been scaled down since 1990. Where once a northern and a southern RAF fighter station maintained 'Q', only Leuchars now does so, assisted by crews and aircraft from the other squadrons on a rotation basis.

Whilst images of crews racing to their interceptors for a 'scramble' are pictorially appealing, they are a sign that NATO has been caught napping. Normally the procedure is more relaxed, thanks to allied surveillance, including the all-seeing E-3 Sentry. Two crews and two Tornado F3s will be on QRA stand-by in hardened shelters close to the runway. Each man must be partly dressed in his flying clothing and stay within a few yards of the shelter during his 24-hour duty period. A rest-room with bed, food and TV/video is provided. Farther south, at Marham or Brize Norton, the crew of a Victor or VC10 tanker is similarly designated.

On warning of a likely unnotified entry in to the UKADR, crews will be placed on a higher alert state, possibly sitting in their cockpits. When the intruder's intentions are known for certain, the fighters will take-off and be controlled by a ground centre (usually Buchan) or a conveniently-placed Sentry AEW1 towards the rendezvous. Should the CIS aircraft remain in the UKADR for some time, the tanker will keep the Tornados on station for several hours.

AIR-TO-AIR REFUELLING

For the RAF, AAR began as a means of deploying bombers world-wide in the 1950s and rapidly spread to tactical forces. Its value in supporting interceptors has been mentioned above but can be reiterated by reference to an incident off the coast of Japan in 1984. Having no tankers, the Japanese were forced to launch 34 fighters at various times to escort two flights of Soviet bombers passing through their airspace. The RAF could have done the same with four Tornados and two VC10s.

From converted bombers, in the seductive shape of the Victor, the RAF is moving to adapted airliners for its tanker force. When the last Victor is withdrawn in October 1993, the regular tanker force will comprise five VC10 K2s, four VC10 K3s and five VC10 K4s which will be augmented, when required, by two TriStar K1s, four TriStar KC1 tanker-transports, six Hercules C1(K)s and eight VC10 C1(K)s. The last-mentioned are best described as 'transports with tanker capability' because, unlike the TriStar, they have insufficient tankage to refuel a pair of fighters *and* carry their support crews and equipment over a long distance. If Argentina again threatened to invade the Falkland Islands, TriStars could bring both two reinforcement aircraft and 250 or so personnel on the same flight.

Here is the distinction between tanker and tanker-transport operations. Day-to-day, tankers are positioned on racetrack-shaped 'tow-lines' over the sea and sparsely-populated areas of land. Interceptor, attack, maritime reconnaissance, AEW and even transport aircraft can book a time-slot to practice refuelling which may, at some future date, become an operational necessity. Additionally, of course, one AAR can almost double the endurance of an aircraft. In one sortie, therefore, a tactical aircraft can accomplish more training without the unnecessary and wasteful transit flight between base and the exercise area. Tankers will routinely be despatched on a 'trail' to take aircraft abroad, such as to the USA for 'Red Flag' or Canada for 'Maple Flag' exercises; to Cyprus or Decimomannu for weapons and combat training; or farther afield on less frequent deployments. In the Gulf War, VC10s, Victors and TriStar K1s were used to support combat missions by Tornados and Jaguars.

Finally, there is 'do-it-yourself' tanking in the form of the 'buddy-buddy' system in which a small refuelling pod is attached to a strike/attack aircraft. Buccaneer S2Bs can be fitted with a FRL Mk20C or 20E pod on the starboard inner pylon to extend their reach in the maritime role, and their replacement Tornado GR1s will have the Sargent-Fletcher 28-300 centreline pod. The RAF acquired 15 of the latter from the German Navy for possible use in the Gulf War and will install them on Tornados when they assume the maritime role from 1993.

HARDENED AIRCRAFT SHELTER OPERATIONS

The HAS first was used by NATO in Europe during the mid-1970s and came to RAF bases in the UK when Honington's first site was opened in November 1981 (for No IX Squadron and its Tornados). The typical site comprises 12 Phase 3 shelters, a Personnel Briefing Facility (PBF) and a Hardened Personnel Shelter (HPS). Two separate sites per station is the norm. The arched HAS is made of reinforced concrete and can protect two Tornado-sized aircraft (three at a squeeze) from a near miss by a 1,000lb bomb. Two flat steel doors are slid back to allow aircraft to leave their HAS and two smaller doors at the rear are opened to allow hot gases to escape through a bifurcated 'chimney' when the aircraft starts its engines. Attached to the side of the building is a similarly reinforced Aerospace Ground Annexe (AGE) with storage space and room for a fuel tanker to drive in. (In RAF Germany, there are many Phase 1 HASs still in use, modified with an AGE, but identifiable by their smaller size — one Tornado or two Jaguars — and the hinged, shell-shaped doors which open beneath a roof overhang, or 'porch'.)

The PBF functions as a squadron HQ. It comprises a main, reinforced and windowless area, plus a 'soft' section, which would be abandoned in wartime, with offices and a rest-room/coffee bar. Air-locks, a decontamination area and air filtering system make the PBF proof against chemical warfare and radioactive dust. Naturally, such

Above:
When threatened with use of chemical or biological weapons, groundcrew must service their aircraft (here a Tornado F3 of No 5 Squadron at Coningsby) wearing helmets and respirators. *Paul Jackson*

Below:
Air-to-ar refuelling is a most useful 'force multiplier'. Studded on its rim with luminous spots, the collapsable drogue is kept open by air pressure as this Phantom refuels from a Hercules C1(K). *Paul Jackson*

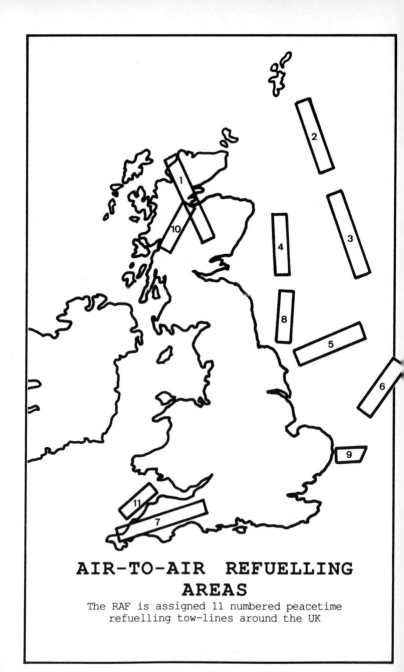

AIR-TO-AIR REFUELLING AREAS

The RAF is assigned 11 numbered peacetime
refuelling tow-lines around the UK

precautions are not taken routinely, but the regular exercises to which all units are submitted ensure that personnel are practiced in NBC (Nuclear, Biological and Chemical) precautions. For aircrew, this means protective body clothing and the Cam Lock AR5 respirator system which covers the entire head before venturing outside. Until plugged into the aircraft's oxygen, aircrew carry a hand-held, battery-powered air filter nicknamed the 'whistling handbag'.

Ground personnel are issued with the same basic type of NBC-protective clothing (the Mk4 'Noddy Suit') and a respirator — originally the S6, but increasingly the new S10. Contrary to popular belief, the HAS is not NBC-proof for the good reason that it has to open its doors for an aircraft to leave. Furthermore, even if the air base had not been under attack, aircraft could return having flown through a cloud of contamination. Off-duty personnel of all ranks would be accommodated in the HPS during war, but this dormitory and feeding area is the one facility which is not used on a day-to-day basis. The HAS and PBF are. This places a strain on maintenance, compared with the traditional system of servicing aircraft in one large hangar (which is, of course, an ideal target for one large bomb). More personnel and tools are needed in the HAS regime, and now that the risk of air attack on the UK is diminished, it may be that some scaling-down of hardened operations could be authorised.

ARMAMENT AND AIR COMBAT PRACTICE

As the age of air-to-air missiles dawned, it was predicted that the cannon would rapidly disappear from interceptor aircraft. Indeed, the later marks of Lightning dispensed with what was regarded as an anachronism — only to have two ADENs fitted to the front of the F6's fuel tanks in middle age. Likewise the Phantom, which in its UK versions had to carry a centreline pod with a six-barrel M61A1 Vulcan fast-firing 20mm weapon. No such mistake has been made with the Tornado F3, which has a 27mm IWKA-Mauser on the starboard side (the GR1 has two) and an advanced air data and sighting computer which makes it highly accurate in close combat.

NATO requires each interceptor pilot to prove his marksmanship annually by putting a specified number of holes through a banner target under controlled conditions of distance and flight pattern. This must be done twice within six consecutive sorties to gain an ACE qualification - not 'ace' as in shooting down five enemy aircraft, but ACE as in Allied Command Europe. The banner is 6ft high and 30ft long, but appears as only 12ft in length because of the acute angle of approach.

The uncertain British weather could disrupt qualification shoots, so each squadron in turn deploys with tanker support to Akrotiri for a three-week APC (Armament Practice Camp). Target towing is by No 100 Squadron, which has a permanent detachment in Cyprus during the shooting season. This used to comprise three Canberras, but 1992 has seen a change to Hawk T1As.

Another yearly excursion is to Valley, in Anglesey. At the Strike Command Air-to-Air Missile Establishment, live rounds are fired at targets towed Jindivik GAF Mk104B drones launched from Llanbedr and monitored by Range Control at Aberporth. Sometimes a Northrop Chukar D2 is used and very occasionally a Beech Stiletto released from under the wing of a specially equipped Canberra. Because of the high cost of even the Sidewinder AAM, squadrons are only allowed up to six missile launches per year, each round carrying a telemetry transmitter to allow later analysis of its performance.

In addition to set camps, squadrons may be called to fire missiles in short notice exercises at Valley. Most heart-stopping of all, QRA fighters will occasionally be launched as if 'for real' and find themselves directed to Cardigan Bay with for an appointment with a Jindivik. In this and the short-notice exercise, live missiles from the squadron's stock are used. Aircraft which use the Sidewinder for self-defence are also visitors to STCAAME: Buccaneer, Harrier, Jaguar and Tornado GR1.

For practice in the skills of air fighting, squadrons deploy to a third location. The NATO Air Combat Manoeuvring Installation at Decimomannu, Sardinia (for short, 'Decci' — pronounced 'deh-chee') is used by a broad variety of allied aircraft, so there are endless possibilities for dissimilar air combat. Each aircraft is fitted with a telemetry pod on one of its Sidewinder launch rails. During air combats off the coast, the pod transmits data to buoys moored at sea and these relay back to base.

After landing, aircrew can replay a computerised recording of their combat on a large screen, allowing them to take-in at leisure lessons which might otherwise have been lost in the heat of the fight. To make the most of the range time available, an aircraft which is 'shot down' is merely frozen-out of combat for an agreed time and then permitted to re-join the fray. Decci provides good weather for most of the year, but those willing to risk the vagaries of the British climate can practice over the similar range in the North Sea. Opened in August 1990 and privately run by British Aerospace, this has already drawn several foreign clients (which fly from RAF Waddington) as well as the RAF. Located 80 miles off Lincolnshire, the NSAR can track simultaneously up to 36 aircraft and 50 missile launch simulations, playing back the results to debriefing facilities at Coningsby, Waddington and USAFB Bentwaters.

UNITED KINGDOM
LOW-LEVEL
CLIMB-OUT
RADAR AREAS

SCOTTISH
MILITARY

BORDER

MIDLAND   EASTERN

LONDON MILITARY
NORTH

LONDON MILITARY SOUTH

LOW-LEVEL FLYING

Low-level flying is an important part of modern offensive air operations and is routinely practiced by RAF aircraft. In the UK, aircraft are restricted to a minimum of 250ft and maximum 450kt (517mph) apart from in three sparsely-populated areas in which the limit is 100ft. Only a small amount of training is conducted in the latter areas, usually in the work-up for squadrons participating in the 'Red Flag' highly realistic combat exercises at Nellis AFB, Nevada, or the similar 'Maple Flag' at CFB Cold Lake. These overseas exercises are valuable training, but the number of European pilots who can participate is necessarily small.

Some of the RAF's low flying is exported to the wastes of Canada, where a detachment of Tornado GR1s is based between April and October under the code name 'Western Vortex'. Crews are flown out to CFB Goose Bay by transport aircraft for short detachments whilst the aircraft, which are donated by several squadrons, remain for the whole season. OLF (Operational Low Flying) is permitted down to 100ft manually or 200ft using the Tornado's automatic terrain-following radar.

BOMBING

Attack aircraft practice bombing both in Canada and the UK, those based in Germany also having their own range at Nordhorn. For reduction of costs, the RAF uses miniature bombs which have the same aerodynamic characteristics as the full-size weapon. The Portsmouth Aviation '3kg' bomb mimics a parachute-retarded 1,000lb bomb or the Hunting BL755 cluster bomb, whilst the same firm's '14kg' bomb parallels a 1,000lb 'slick' which may be thrown four miles in a lofting or 'toss-bombing' pull-up type of attack. A flash and smoke cartridge in the bomb is detonated on impact to assist range officers to plot its position. Tornados use the ML Aviation CBLS200 (Carrier, Bomb, Light Stores) practice-bomb carrier, but most other types of aircraft have the older, but similar CBLS100.

Weapons ranges in the UK include Tain and Rosehearty in Scotland; Cowden, Donna Nook, Wainfleet and Holbeach on the East Coast; and Jurby, Isle of Man. For practice in use of electronic warfare equipment, aircraft will fly through the training area at Spadeadam, Northumbria, close to which is a dummy airfield on the Otterburn training area, complete with withdrawn aircraft as targets. Live bombing, though rare, takes place on Garvey Island, off the northwest coast of Scotland. Other ranges are used by the MoD for weapons development and at Pembrey by Hawks for students' training.

When full-size bombs are seen beneath an aircraft, they will usually be blue-painted, concrete-filled practice weapons. Standard RAF bomb is the 1,000lb medium-case high explosive with Mark numbers ranging from 13 to 22. Typical weight with a Hunting Mk114 'slick' (aerodynamic) tail fin assembly for lofting attacks is 1,030lb. Retarded by a Hunting Mk117 parachute tail for low-level delivery, this increases to 1,130lb. Precision delivery is achieved by attaching a Texas Instruments Paveway II laser guidance kit to the Mk13/22 series, this comprising a CPU-123/B nose assembly plus tail-fins, increasing total weight to 1,210lb. For laser guidance, Buccaneers use the Westinghouse Pave Spike system (known to the USAF as AN/ASQ-153), including the AN/AVQ-23E designator pod on the port inner pylon. Tornado GR1s will employ Ferranti's TIALD designator (port under-fuselage pylon) which was pulled out of the laboratory in 1991 for successful use in the Gulf War and is now completing its development.

Still in stock are the Mks 1 and 2 bombs of nominal 540lb weight. Free-fall versions weigh 570lb, whilst the Hunting Mk118 retarding tail increases this to 620lb. Hunting also makes cluster-bomb units (CBUs), of which the BL755 (RAF designation L1) is fitted to Jaguars, Harriers and occasionally Tornado GR1s. It weighs 610lb in original form and 582lb as the Improved BL755. For cratering runways and laying small anti-personnel mines to hamper repair, Tornado GR1s are fitted with two Hunting JP233 bomblet dispensers (RAF type L2) weighing 5,148lb each. The MATRA 155 launcher for eighteen 68mm rockets is used occasionally by Harriers and weighs 400lb loaded. For the Gulf War, Jaguars were armed with Bristol Aerospace (Canada) LAU-5003B/A pods containing nineteen CRV-7 high-velocity rockets, for a loaded weight of 530lb per pod. Nuclear weapons are the 100 kilotonne WE177B for Tornado GR1s and other versions of the same device for Buccaneers and Nimrods. Buccaneers carry a smaller WE177 (originally — at least — code-named 'Red Beard') whilst the Nimrod's weapon is configured as a depth-charge.

FLYING CLOTHING AND SURVIVAL EQUIPMENT

In an average year, the RAF will lose 17 aircraft and two helicopters in accidents. The crew's chances of survival in an emergency are improved by ejection seats (in most aircraft) and the yellow helicopters of Nos 22 and 202 Squadrons, but carefully designed flying clothing and survival equipment also play an important part.

FLYING CLOTHING

● **Helmet** ('Bone dome') Types in use are Mk3C and Mk4A, with the Alpha helmet in prospect as Mk10 — the last-mentioned, like Mk4, having a cut-away back to assist all-round scanning by the 'Mk1 eyeball'. All have a hinged transparent visor and a sun-visor.

● **Oxygen mask** Type P with a large face-piece and Type Q, small. External appearance identical.

● **Underwear** Long Johns ('Drawers, Aircrew, Long, Cotton Ribbed') and Mk2 T-shirt; augmented in cold weather by a heat-retaining, one-piece inner coverall or 'Bunny Suit' — Mk1 knitted or Mk3 of woollen composites.

● **Flying Suit** Coverall of Nomex flame-retardant material, Mk14 (various pocket configurations). Includes sheath for Mk3 knife.

● **Anti-G trousers** (popularly, but incorrectly termed a 'G-suit'). Normally Mk2A or (for Tornado) Mk4, both worn externally, but Mk6C goes under the flying suit.

● **Immersion suit** Winter-wear, when sea temperatures are fatally cold. Mk1 internal, but normally Mk10 external (over all the above-mentioned clothing). Tornado crew wear Mk10A with added neck seal. For comfort it is made of open-weave material which expands to become liquid-proof on entering water.

● **Life preserver** The inflatable life-jacket — also containing an emergency beacon — far removed from the simple 'Mae West' of World War 2. Mk20 or Mk30 versions, but Tornado crew have Mk27S or 27SA with open-work sleeves to support D-rings for the arm-restraining cords associated with Martin-Baker Mk10 ejection seat.

● **Gloves** Mk2, leather.

● **Boots** Aircrew 1965 Pattern or Lightweight, with Mk2 Terryloop socks or Mk3 immersion socks.

Additionally, on active service, the following items are added or substituted:
Respirator NBC No 5 ('AR5'); Gloves NBC Mk2; Coverall NBC Mk1; Socks NBC Mk2. Personal armament Walther 7.65mm pistol and holster.

On ejection, the occupant is automatically separated from his (or — since a Harrier T4 crash in September 1991 — her) seat, but remains connected to a Personal Survival Pack containing an inflatable dinghy and a host of ingenious survival aids. To prepare for such an emergency, aircrew are given courses at the School of Combat Survival (originally Mount Batten, but moved to St Mawgan in September 1992). Outdoor exercises will include escape and evasion, together with practice in trapping wild animals and living off the land (for those with strong enough stomachs).

BATTLE DAMAGE REPAIR

As a means of increasing the effective strength of the RAF on the second and subsequent days of a war, techniques have been developed of rapidly repairing damage caused by enemy defences to aircraft in action. The centre of research was the Battle Damage Repair School at Abingdon, although No 431 MU at Brüggen deserves credit as another pioneer of such work. BDR aims to repair an aircraft in 8-12 hours — compared with weeks or months to do the same job with manufacturer's parts. The only rule is that the aircraft must be safe to

Right:
PERSONAL SURVIVAL PACK
In addition to an inflatable dinghy, the ejection seat of a combat aircraft includes a pack of survival aids for use at sea or on the land. The Phantom's Type ZD Mk3 contains the following, although contents are similar for most types of aircraft. Two No 1 Mk2 hand-held flares, three de-salting kits (two pints each), knife and sharpening stone, waterproof matches, an edible candle (sic), scarf, wire-saw, compass, animal snare, fishing kit, spare socks and gloves, Mk3 pyrotechnic pistol kit and flares, seawater-activated battery, first-aid kit and 'Flying Rations, Emergency, Mk4' — better described as butterscotch sweets, the tin for which has hand-holds so it can double as a small cooking container.

FLYING CLOTHING
Left:

What the well-dressed pilot is wearing this summer season. Representing Phantom aircrew in NBC-protective dress, this pilot has a Mk4A helmet with visor protected by a cloth anti-scratch cover; AR5 respirator system comprising an air-tight rubber head cover with integral oxygen mask and transparent face-piece; Mk20 life-preserver; Mk14 flying suit; Mk2A anti-G trousers; rubber Mk2 NBC gloves; and hand-held, battery-powered ventilator to be used until plugged into the aircraft's oxygen system. Note that velcro-backed squadron badges have been removed from the flying suit as would be the case in wartime.

Below:

LIFE PRESERVER Mk30

More than just water-wings. The life preserver contains a whistle, list of emergency signals to SAR aircraft, a heliograph, water-activated battery and light, a gas cylinder (for inflation), razor blade, personal locator beacon (and radio aerial), basic first-aid kit and a pack of mini-flares with a pencil-shaped launcher.

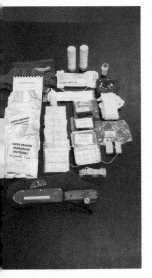

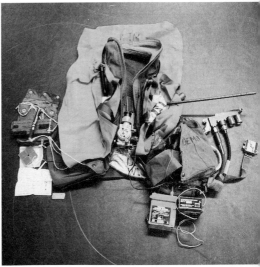

fly afterwards; within that proviso, ingenious methods are used to patch shell-holes, repair control-rods and splice electrical wiring with any materials to hand.

Combat stations have BDR airframes in the form of aircraft which would otherwise have been scrapped at the end of their operational lives. They serve as subjects for training and for Taceval exercises, when an examiner will declare a squadron aircraft to be unserviceable until a representative repair has been undertaken on the BDR airframe.

TACEVALS

Tacevals (Tactical Evaluations) are part of a NATO assessment procedure for every front-line air base. They come in two parts, the first of which is a no-notice call-out at which squadrons must bring 70% of their aircraft

Battle Damage Repair is most valuable in maximising assets in wartime. Cut wires will be spliced and a patch riveted over the buckled metal once the edges have been dressed. *RAF Abingdon*

to readiness within 12hr. Part two, some days later, is a broader test of base security and defence, BDR capability, repair of airfield damage (see Territorial Army in the next chapter), medical care, and similar aspects. The international team of examiners awards points in each category and brings any weaknesses to the attention of the station commander.

NATO EXERCISES

Air defence forces have the opportunity to combat simulated raids on the UK during regular exercises, in which other air forces and RAF strike/attack aircraft operating from the continent lay the role of attackers. Largest of these is 'Elder Forest', held in the spring of even-numbered years. Similar, but smaller, is 'Elder Joust', in the spring and autumn, the former cancelled when clashing with 'Elder Forest'. Exercises last a week, including three main flying days. Also well known, but different in its purpose, the twice-yearly 'Mallet Blow' brings foreign visitors to the UK to operate alongside the RAF against the Otterburn and Spadeadam weapons ranges.

6 RAF Regiment, Reserves and Auxiliaries

Far from all RAF personnel are concerned with the immediate task of getting an aircraft into the air. Others are one step removed from such work, although their activities are no less vital to the efficient and safe operation of every RAF station. This chapter examines the RAF Regiment, Fire Service, Royal Auxilliary Air Force, RAF Volunteer Reserve and units of the Army and Territorial Army.

ROYAL AUXILIARY AIR FORCE

Having fought with distinction in World War 2, the RAuxAF flying squadrons converted to jet fighters, but disbanded in 1957. Only a small number of ground-based units then remained, including the Maritime HQs, formed as co-ordination centres in November-December 1959. Numbers were increased from 1979 onwards with addition of squadrons to the RAF Regiment and with an Air Movements Squadron in 1982.

On 1 April 1986 the RAF began a trial to assess the practicability of placing RAuxAF personnel as aircrew aboard VC10s and Nimrods. This proved to be successful in the case of Nimrod Air Electronics Officers and the RAuxAF was thus able to play a front-line role — albeit small — in the 1991 Gulf War.

Current units of this part-time force are listed below. An explanation of RAuxAF Regiment Field Squadron roles will be found under the RAF Regiment heading. Traditionally, squadrons are named for the area from which they draw their volunteers.

● No 1 Maritime HQ *City of Hertford* — Northwood
● No 2 Maritime HQ *City of Edinburgh* — Pitrievie Castle
● No 3 Maritime HQ *County of Devon* — St Mawgan (Mountbatten up to September 1992)

● No 4624 *County of Oxford* (Movements) Sqn — Brize Norton
● No 4626 *County of Wiltshire* (Aeromedical Evacuation Sqn) — Hullavington (to new location in 1993)

Royal Auxiliary Air Force Regiment
● No 1310 Wing, HQ: Catterick
 No 2620 *County of Norfolk* Field Sqn — Marham (No 1 Group)
 No 2622 *Highland* Field Sqn — Lossiemouth (No 18 Group)
 No 2623 *East Anglian* Field Sqn — Honington (No 1 Group)
 No 2624 *County of Oxford* Field Sqn — Brize Norton (No 1 Group)
 No 2625 *County of Cornwall* Field Sqn — St Mawgan (No 1 Group)
● No 1339 Wing, HQ: Waddington
 No 2503 *County of Lincoln* Field Sqn — Waddington (No 11 Group)
 No 2729 *City of Lincoln* Sqn — Waddington (No 11 Group)
 No 2890 Sqn — Waddington

RAF VOLUNTEER RESERVE

It is often forgotten that the majority of those who were conscripted into the RAF during World War 2 became members of the RAFVR, not the 'regular' RAF. Now the VR staffs just four Flights, although there are a further 3,300 unpaid members of the RAFVR (Training) who operate Air Training Corps squadrons and the associated AEFs and VGSs.

● **No 7006 Flight** — High Wycombe — (intelligence)
● **No 7010 Flight** — Wyton — (photographic interpretation)
● **No 7630 Flight** — Ashford — (interrogation)
● **No 7644 Flight** — Uxbridge — (public relations)

ROYAL AIR FORCE REGIMENT

Formed in February 1941 to provide defence of RAF aerodromes, the regiment has a similar role today, using both SAMs and surface transport — plus a few AA guns. The Commandant-General of the Regiment is also responsible for the RAF Police, Security Services and Fire Service, but control of all four is devolved to Commands and stations. All personnel receive initial training at the Regiment Depot at Catterick.

Short-Range Air Defence Squadrons
SHORAD squadrons are equipped principally with the BAe Rapier surface-to-air missile and tasked with destroying enemy aircraft attacking airfields. The exceptions are Nos 2729 and 2890 Auxiliary Squadrons (see RAuxAF, above), armed with Oerlikon anti-aircraft cannon and associated Contraves Skyguard radar, both captured from Argentina in the 1982 Falklands War. No 2729 formed 1 April 1985 and was later split to establish No 2890. No 6 Wing mans Rapiers bought by the US Government for defence of USAF bases in England. For administrative reasons, its squadrons are

based on RAF stations in peacetime. All Rapier squadrons spend a month at firing camp on South Uist, Hebrides, each year.

- **No 15 Squadron**   Leeming (No 11 Group)
- **No 26 Squadron**   Laarbruch (RAF Germany)
- **No 27 Squadron**   Leuchars (No 11 Group)
- **No 37 Squadron**   Brüggen (RAF Germany)
- **No 48 Squadron**   Lossiemouth (No 11 Group)
- **No 63 Squadron**   Gütersloh (RAF Germany)

(RAF Germany squadrons were controlled by No 4 Wing at Wildenrath until its disbandment in 1991; No 16 Squadron disbanded at Wildenrath in April 1992; No 63 disbands October 1992)

No 6 Wing, HQ: West Raynham
- **No 19 Squadron**   Brize Norton (UASFBs Fairford and Upper Heyford)
- **No 20 Squadron**   Honington (USAFBs Alconbury, Woodbridge and Bentwaters)
- **No 66 Squadron**   West Raynham (USAFBs Mildenhall and Lakenheath)

(No 66 is first to be equipped with Rapier Mk2, in 1991)

Light Armoured and Field Squadrons
Equipment for air base perimeter defence by Light Armoured Squadrons comprises machine guns, mortars, anti-tank rockets and the range of Alvis armoured and tracked vehicles. Each unit has 15 FV101 Scorpion reconnaissance vehicles (76mm gun); six FV103 Spartan armoured personnel carriers; one FV105 Sultan command vehicle; and one F106 Samson recovery vehicle. The RAuxAF Regiment Field

Squadrons (No 2620, etc — see above) have LandRovers and hand-held weapons only. (No 5 Wing at Hullavington and co-located No 15 (LA) Squadron both disbanded on 31 July 1990.) The Queen's Colour Squadron (formed 1 November 1960) has ceremonial duties whilst in the UK.

No 3 Wing, HQ: Catterick:
- **No 2 (Parachute) Squadron**   War base: Gütersloh
- **No 51 (LA) Squadron**   War base: Brüggen

No 33 Wing, HQ: Gütersloh:
- **No 1 (LA) Squadron**, Laarbruch   War role: Harrier Force defence

(On 1 April 1992 No 2 Squadron arrived from Hullavington and No 58 (LA) Squadron disbanded. The Support Flight of

the Regiment Depot at Catterick has a war role assisting in defence of the Harrier Force in Germany)

HQ Strike Command:
- **No 34 (LA) Squadron**, Akrotiri   War role: RAF Germany
- **Queen's Colour Squadron**, Uxbridge   War role: RAF Germany helicopter force

(No 34 Squadron's armoured vehicles are stockpiled in Germany — it uses LandRovers in Cyprus; the QCS has no combat transport in the UK and is assigned LandRovers in Germany)

Air base security
Two forms of base perimeter security are practiced. In wartime, the RAF regiment in its vehicles would patrol the area surrounding a combat station whilst all ranks and

RAF Regiment squadrons take turns to spend three months on the Falkland Islands manning Rapier sites defending Mount Pleasant. Elements are the 7.62mm machine gun, DN181 Blindfire radar, control officer with manual override 'pointing stick' and launch unit. *Paul Jackson*

trades were armed with hand weapons to defend points within the boundary. In peacetime, all stations have to be patrolled against a terrorist threat. The first sight greeting a visitor arriving at the gate of an RAF installation will often be an L85 (SA80) rifle pointing at them from a slit in a Yarnold Bunker (named for Sqn Ldr Jed Yarnold, RAF Regiment, who devised the system of modifying mains sewer pipes to cheap, but effective miniature pill-boxes, during the recent re-construction of Leeming).

Augmenting basic training at Swinderby, all new non-commissioned arrivals at an RAF station begin their posting with an average

Above:
The main RAF fire appliances (l-r), Mk11 Primary 1, Mk10 Primary 2 and TACR Mk2 pose by a Hunter training airframe at the Fire Services Central Training Establishment, Manston. *Paul Jackson*

Left:
The four-round Rapier launch unit. *Paul Jackson*

Below:

With a 'Bomb Disposal' badge on its turret, Wattisham's Alvis Scorpion is driven by personnel in full NBC protective kit. *Paul Jackson*

Bottom:

Moving equipment of airport size is needed for the RAF's largest aircraft, as exemplified by this Reliance Mercury tractor unit manoeuvring a Sentry AEW1 at Waddington. *Paul Jackson*

of three days of lectures by the resident Regiment officer and his staff on rifle drill and shooting, first aid, security, basic fire-fighting and other aspects of RAF life. Three or four times per year, airmen up to Flight Sergeant rank have a short refresher course and target practice on the station rifle range before beginning a week of base guarding duties, assisting the RAF police at the gate and making regular rounds of the camp and airfield. Since 1 April 1984, airwomen have been required to qualify in the use of rifles, but they do not undertake day-to-day guarding duties. Previously, those to be given rifles in wartime were only half-jokingly referred to as 'cooks and clerks'. With many such trades now sub-contracted to civilian firms, the burden of base security falls on a smaller number of uniformed personnel.

ROYAL AIR FORCE FIRE SERVICE

Administered by the RAF Regiment, the RAFFS also employs locally-based civilians at certain stations. All training is conducted at Manston by the Fire Services Central Training Establishment (formed 1 January 1989 on addition of elements formerly at Catterick). As expected, the FSCTE has a range of instructional airframes — some for burning, some not — but its training aids reflect the fact that it is responsible for all types of fire on RAF stations, including domestic incidents in married quarters. For that reason, a

small fire staff must remain on duty even when flying has ceased for the day.

Provision of vehicles is according to the types of aircraft operating from or visiting a station. A typical base would have one Mk10 Primary 2 fire tender, one Mk11 Primary 1 and one TACR Mk2 (Truck, Airfield Crash Rescue) Rapid Intervention Vehicle. Whilst the Mks 10 and 11 resemble civilian fire engines (except for the foam monitor on top), the TACR is a six-wheel RangeRover designed to race to the scene of an aircraft accident. Stations regularly receiving the large TriStar have small turntable ladders added to the Mk11s, whilst at Mount Pleasant, Falkland islands, the terrain also demands a Haggelunds BV206 over-snow tracked vehicle towing a rescue trailer.

ARMY AND TERRITORIAL ARMY

The Royal Engineers are tasked with assisting RAF Germany to construct forward operating bases and keep permanent stations operational in wartime. In the former category, four squadrons, including one normally based in the UK, would prepare sites for Harriers and Chinooks/Pumas. A further three home-based squadrons are assigned to airfield damage repair at the 'Clutch' bases. Their work would be undertaken in conjunction with RAF personnel trained in disposal of unexploded bombs and aided by two Gazelle HT3s detached from No 2 FTS (painted in camouflage) which would reconnoitre the station after a raid.

● No 10 Field Squadron; No 48 Field Squadron*	Harrier Force
● No 11 Field Squadron; No 32 Field Squadron	Helicopter Force
● No 52 Field Squadron (Construction)*	Brüggen
● No 50 Field Squadron (Construction)*	Laarbruch
(Wildenrath was assigned No 53 Field Squadron*)	* based in the UK

On 26 March 1983, No 277 Field Squadron formed as the first Territorial Army (TA) unit dedicated to damage repair. The part-time volunteer units comprise about 84 men, rolls of metal matting to lay over large repaired holes, stocks of quick-drying concrete and a fleet of contractor's plant. Typically the latter comprises: three earth-movers; one JCB; six earth-carrying trucks; one excavator; two graders; four general-purpose trucks; four Volvo fork-lift trucks; two Alvis Saracen armoured reconnaissance vehicles; two motor-rollers; and, three Coles cranes used as compactors. A full-time army Major is in command, and the 27 days per year of training include repair of holes pur-

posely dug into disused sections of taxiway and runway. Units are as below, the full title of each being Field Squadron (Airfield Damage Repair) Royal Engineers (Volunteers).

● No 212 Squadron,	RE	Wattisham
● No 216 Squadron,	RE	Marham
● No 218 Squadron,	RE	Honington
● No 219 Squadron,	RE	Coningsby
● No 234 Squadron,	RE	Leeming
● No 267 Squadron,	RE	Waddington
● No 277 Squadron,	RE	Leuchars
● No 236 Squadron,	RE	Kinloss

(No 218 will disband in 1993 and its equipment is to be transferred to Lossiemouth to permit formation of No 237 Squadron)

7 Radars for control and defence

Aircraft and ground radar are inseparable; at least one rotating antenna will be seen at every RAF flying station. Additional installations elsewhere are responsible for air safety in busy training areas and yet others watch over the approaches to UK shores for the approach of unannounced intruders. In looking first at the local control of an aerodrome, the opportunity will be taken to describe the layout and markings of an average RAF airfield.

Before proceeding, however, it is as well to re-define terms which have become blurred by recent mis-use. 'Airfield' is a landing area for aircraft; 'aerodrome' is an airfield plus its associated hangars, workshops and accommodation. The latter is referred to as an 'RAF station' (or USAF base), but this term should include the married quarters and any other related areas belonging to the RAF. Conversely, of course, stations may be devoid of an airfield if their role is storage, administration or communications.

LOCAL AIR TRAFFIC CONTROL

The control tower
In overall command of the Senior Air Traffic Control Officer (SATCO) — of Squadron Leader or Wing Commander rank — the tower has two separate, but closely connected functions: aerodrome control and radar approach. At all times, the assistant SATCO or a supervising officer will be present and responsible for both operations. Personnel are trained by the Central Air Traffic Control School at Shawbury.

In the glass top to the tower are the Aerodrome Controller (ADC) — ranking between Sergeant and Flight Lieutenant — an assistant and the Duty Aircrew Officer (a member of one of the resident flying units). They control all activity on the airfield (including vehicles); aircraft in the visual circuit (up to 3,000ft or five to six miles) and give clearances for radar approaches.

It is in the darkened Radar Approach Room below that talk-downs are conducted. Here are three Surveillance Radar Controllers, two Talk-down Controllers, an assistant and a switchboard operator. Surveillance radar is usually a Plessey Watchman positioned in one corner of the airfield and used to watch all aircraft within 40 miles, although its maximum range is double that

figure. Talk-down controllers use a three-dimensional, twin-screen display provided by the Precision Approach Radar (PAR). The latter looks nothing like a traditional radar, but is a box-shaped construction half-way down the main runway which may be swung a turntable through 180° to view aircraft approaching from either direction.

Not to be forgotten, the Runway Controller — normally a Corporal — has an observation position in a specially designed vehicle parked at the touch-down point (usually on the pilot's left) of the runway in use. Following a change of wind direction, he will drive to the opposite end and plug in to the electricity supplies and land-lines there. The Runway Controller is responsible for activity in his vicinity, including the safety of aircraft taking off and landing. Those taking off are checked to ensure all safety-flags are removed, whilst aircraft on the approach are examined through binoculars — and not just for the obvious omission of failing to lower the undercarriage. Any aircraft entering a dangerous situation will be signalled with a red flare.

Outside the control tower is the airfield identification code and Signals Square. The latter is rarely used, but in former times would convey to pilots by means of symbols what is now transmitted by radio. The two-letter code in white concrete laid into grass is at night repeated in Morse Code by the red Aerodrome Identification Beacon located on a building or unobstructed part of the airfield and by the radio-aid Non-Directional Beacon (if installed). Codes are far from cryptic — such as LM for Lossiemouth and SM for St Mawgan — but are unrelated to the four-letter international aerodrome codes used for flight-planning: EGQS and EGDG respectively, for those cited.

Area controls
Aircraft leaving the aerodrome will often be handed-over to a military radar service which will ensure that the skies are kept a safe distance from other traffic, civil and military. With the closure of Midland Radar at North Luffenham in January 1990 there was a re-organisation of area controls. The present situation is:

● **London Military Radar** at West Drayton
● **Eastern Radar** at West Drayton

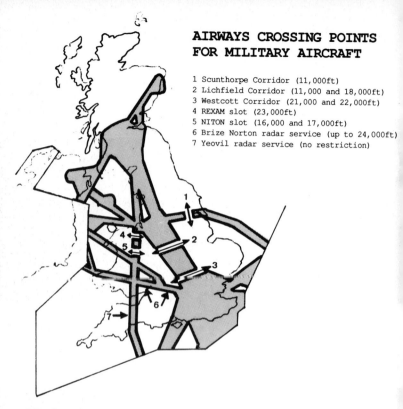

AIRWAYS CROSSING POINTS FOR MILITARY AIRCRAFT

1 Scunthorpe Corridor (11,000ft)
2 Lichfield Corridor (11,000 and 18,000ft)
3 Westcott Corridor (21,000 and 22,000ft)
4 REXAM slot (23,000ft)
5 NITON slot (16,000 and 17,000ft)
6 Brize Norton radar service (up to 24,000ft)
7 Yeovil radar service (no restriction)

● **Border Radar** at Watton
● **Scottish Military Radar** at Prestwick

The headquarters bear no relationships to the location of radars, as the Civil Aviation Authority's network is used for military control.

To simplify crossing of civil airways, certain corridors and 'slots' are reserved for military aircraft at specified heights. Examples are the Scunthorpe corridor, North-South across Blue 1; Lichfield corridor and Westcott corridor, both East-West through the main London-Scotland airways group; and the REXAM and NITON slots, East-West through Amber 25.

At lower levels, where radar coverage is limited by distance, an advisory service is provided by civil airport and military aerodrome radars which covers nearly the whole of England. Pilots participating in this voluntary Lower Airspace Radar Service contact Surveillance Radar Controllers in individual control towers and are kept clear of known conflicting traffic. A more detailed explanation of procedures will be found in *abc Air Traffic Control*, published by Ian Allan Ltd.

Designated airfields are kept open 24hr per day for emergency use by military or civil aircraft. Known as MEDAs (Military Emergency Diversion Airfields) they are kept staffed and lit throughout the night and constantly monitor the international distress frequencies of 121.5mHz and 243.0mHz. Current MEDAs are Manston (Kent), Leuchars (Fife), St Mawgan (Cornwall) and Brize Norton (Oxfordshire). Until 1 March 1991 Kinloss, Leeming, Lyneham, Valley, Waddington and Wattisham also had this status — the Lyneham commitment having been taken-up by Brize Norton.

Additionally, Kinloss, Leeming, Marham Valley and Waddington remain open until midnight between Monday and Thursday and to 18.00 on Friday to accept emergency landings by hook-equipped tactical

Above:
Local control at Wattisham. Plt Off Donna Manley and SAC Chris Young are responsible for all aircraft movements within five miles and up to 3,000ft. *Paul Jackson*

Below:
In the darkened Radar Approach Room, a computer-generated radar picture from the Plessey Watchman depicts the Suffolk and Essex coasts. *Paul Jackson*

aircraft undertaking night flying. In the summer months, Waddington is open to 04.00 to provide cover for Support Command training aircraft.

AIRFIELD INSTALLATIONS AND MARKINGS

Most current RAF stations were constructed in the 1930s with permanent buildings and a grass airfield which was upgraded with three concrete runways during World War 2. Arrival of jet aircraft usually implied an increase in length for at least one runway — wherever possible, that facing the prevailing (westerly) wind. V-bomber bases were designated Class 'A' airfields with even longer, 9,000ft runways. Today, it is rare for a station to use more than one runway, and the others will probably have been broken up, used for parking or allowed to deteriorate. In wartime, straight stretches of taxyway can act as emergency runways.

Parking areas are connected to the runway by taxyways, which are lit at night with blue lights on both sides. At 225ft from the runway's edge is a compulsory stop line for aircraft and vehicles known as the Holding Position. From there, aircraft receive permission to taxy to the runway by radio; vehicles obey ground-level traffic lights. On a board by the Holding Point, and also painted in large characters on the runway, is the Runway Numbering. Two digits are used, giving the magnetic heading to the nearest ten degrees and omitting the final nought; for example a runway direction between 265° and 274° would be marked '27'. Of course, the magnetic variation is just that — a variation — and its slow movement has caused the re-designation of some runways. Naturally, at the opposite end, the runway is called by another name, the difference always being 18 (in other words, 180°): 08/26, 09/27, 10/28, etc.

Heading towards landing, aircraft will first overfly the approach lighting: white lights on poles of increasing height which are illuminated in poor weather or at night. Like most airfield lighting its intensity can be infinitely controlled. Major runways have directional (headlamp-like) approach lights in the form of a centreline and five crossbars ('CL5B'); minor ones are two-bar ('CL2B'). The runway threshold is marked with green lights at ground level; the far end with red. Most major runways have side-lighting of two forms: uni-directional and omni-directional. The former is a high

intensity white light shining towards the landing aircraft; the latter a low intensity white covered by a glass dome. Minor runways possess only 'omnis'.

Immediately beyond the threshold lights are the Threshold Markings in the form of broad white stripes — inevitably nicknamed 'piano keys' followed by the Runway Numbering. If touching-down at the start of the concrete would mean a dangerously low approach over a main road or obstruction, there is a Displaced Threshold some distance along the runway. Broad centreline arrows lead to the marking of a white line crossing the runway and emphasised by four white chevrons.

In the final stages of approach, pilots refer for orientation to two blocks of four lights set slightly back from the threshold to the right and left of the runway. These, the Precision Approach Path Indicators (PAPI), are so aligned that they show white if the aircraft is too high (3.5°, or above) and red if too low (2.5°, or below). When on the optimum 3° glidepath, the pilot sees the inner pair of each block red and the outer pair white. To the ground observer more than a few yards away, they naturally appear red.

In the event a brake — and, if applicable, braking-parachute — failure, the pilot of a small- or medium-sized aircraft will have one or two safety features in his favour. Tactical aircraft have arrestor hooks which, unlike those of naval aircraft, are spring loaded and can not be retracted at will (unless, of course, they are were designed for the navy, like the Phantom and Buccaneer). Runways will have two cables stretched across them at least 1,300ft from each end and supported on rubber grommets. These are connected to a Rotary Hydraulic Arrestor Gear (RHAG, or 'rag') set into the ground and operating in the same manner as the systems found on aircraft carriers. Also available — and used, for example, at Wattisham — is the G+W 'Portarrest' Portable Arrestor Gear (PAG) mounted on a pair of wheeled trailers firmly secured to the ground. Boards by the side of the runway mark the RHAG and others, along its whole length, display a single number counting-down the thousands of feet to the runway's end.

The back-up for RHAG/PAG is the arrestor barrier at the extreme end of the runway. Generally, this is a Befab Mk12A or 12B, the designation abbreviated to RAF A or RAF B. Made of elastic material, the barrier will stop

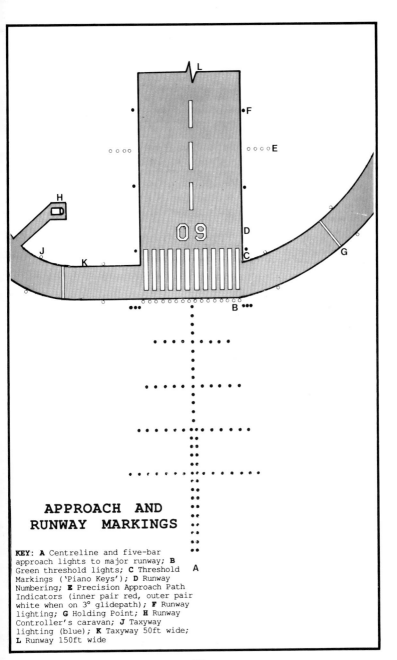

APPROACH AND
RUNWAY MARKINGS

KEY: A Centreline and five-bar approach lights to major runway; **B** Green threshold lights; **C** Threshold Markings ('Piano Keys'); **D** Runway Numbering; **E** Precision Approach Path Indicators (inner pair red, outer pair white when on 3° glidepath); **F** Runway lighting; **G** Holding Point; **H** Runway Controller's caravan; **J** Taxyway lighting (blue); **K** Taxyway 50ft wide; **L** Runway 150ft wide a slow moving fighter with little damage, but it is lowered when there is a take-off or a large aircraft is landing — it being of little help to a Hercules, for example.

AIR DEFENCE RADARS

Assisted by the newly-arrived Boeing Sentry AEW1, ground radar stations and control centres are responsible for the air defence of the United Kingdom and its coastal waters. By agreement with its allies, the RAF covers most of NATO Early Warning Area 12, its 'beat' being known as the UK Air Defence Region (UKADR). Covering 750,000 square miles and stretching 1,100 miles from north to south, the UKADR includes all of UK land, plus most of the airspace between southern Norway and Iceland. It is divided into two parts, of which Sector 1 is the airspace north of 55° N, and Sector 2, the remainder. Tornado F3s on QRA stand ready to investigate aircraft transiting the ADR which have not filed a flight-plan.

Main control centres are underground, principal of which is the Air Defence Operations Centre at Strike Command HQ, High Wycombe; its reserve is the Secondary ADOC at Bentley Priory, Stanmore — the home of No 11 Group. Sectors 1 and 2 each have a Sector Operations Centre (SOC), controlling a number of Control and Reporting Centres (CRC) or Control and Reporting Points (CRP) with associated radars and facilities to speak to interceptor aircraft. Reporting Points (RP) have only a radar.

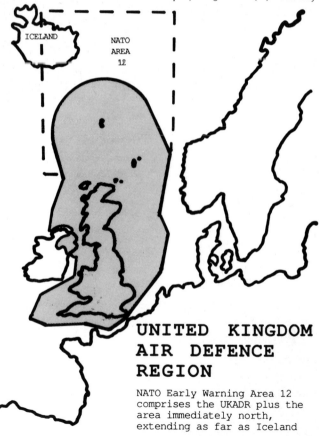

UNITED KINGDOM AIR DEFENCE REGION

NATO Early Warning Area 12 comprises the UKADR plus the area immediately north, extending as far as Iceland

KEY

■ Military installation

● Civil Aviation Authority radar (providing data for RAF low-level climb-out control)

Saxa Vord (CRP+RP)

Faroe Islands (CRP+RP)

Stornoway

Benbecula (CRP+RP)

Buchan (SOC, CRC+RP)

Tiree ●

Lowther Hill

Boulmer (CRC+RP)

Great Dun Fell

Staxton Wold (RP)

Claxby ●

Neatishead (SOC, CRC+RP)

Clee Hill ●

Debden

Heathrow ●

Ash (CRC)

Mount Gabriel (Republic of Ireland)

Burrington ●

Pease Pottage ●

Ventnor

Portreath (CRP+RP)

AIR DEFENCE RADARS

Many of these installations are co-located and it is interesting to note that the CRP+RP on the Faroe Islands is entirely controlled and operated by Denmark. Controllers are trained by the School of Fighter Control, Boulmer. Unit disposition now is:

● **Sector 1 (Buchan)**

Faroes	CRP+RP
Saxa Vord	CRP+RP
Benbecula	CRP+RP
Buchan	CRC+RP and SOC
Boulmer	CRC+RP and reserve SOC
Staxton Wold	RP

(The former RP at Bishop's Court, Northern Ireland, has disbanded)

● **Sector 2 (Neatishead)**

Neatishead	CRC+RP and SOC
Ash	CRC and reserve SOC
Portreath	CRP+RP

In 1977, the RAF began a 10-year improvement programme for No 11 Group's assets, although some aspects have taken longer to come on line. In addition to refurbishment of underground CRCs, radars have been replaced and a new computerised communications network installed. The latter, Improved UK Air Defence Ground Environment, gained initial operational capability in mid-1992. Also delayed is JTIDS (Joint Tactical Information Distribution System), which is a secure net operating between ground stations, ships and aircraft. The Sentry AEW1 has interim JTIDS capability, but no terminals have yet been installed in Tornado F3s, as originally planned.

Replacing the static (and thus vulnerable to air attack) radars at the RPs are mobile units in the form of four Marconi Type 91 Martellos (S723) delivered from 1987; two General Electric Type 92s (TPS-592s) from 1984; and six Plessey-ITT Type 93s (AR 320s) to complete the programme in 1988-89. A further Type 91 is based in the Faroes and contributes to the UKADR, whilst a Westinghouse AN/TPS-43 captured from Argentina is at the Buchan RP. Mobile radars are regularly deployed from the home base with, for example, Boulmer's Type 91 at Brunton and its Type 92 at Ouston — both sites former airfields. These locations would be changed in wartime for other pre-surveyed positions.

Also available, if required, is the Strike Command Mobile Radar Reserve in the form of No 144 Signals Unit at Ty Croes, near Valley, with commitments including overseas deployment. In 1989, the unit's Type 99 radar was assembled at Kuantan, Malaysia, to take part in a local exercise. (Also abroad, and thus not directly concerned with this description, are a Type 90/Martello S713 in Cyprus; and two Type 94/Plessey AR3Ds and two Type 97/Marconi Srs 600s all in the Falkland Islands.)

Additionally supplying data to the UKADR is the Ballistic Missile Early Warning System installation at Fylingdales. Here, the famous three 'golfballs', each covering an AN/FPS-49 radar are in process of replacement by a single AN/FPS-115 'Pave Paws' installation in the form of a sawn-off pyramid 25ft high. As noted previously, NATO air defences are permanently declared to the Alliance and any unit can call-up information from the RASP (Recognised Air-Sea Picture) covering the entire NATO area and fed by all its sensors.

Now absent from the order of battle is the Royal Observer Corps. A direct-reporting element of Strike Command, the Corps was a valuable aircraft-monitoring asset in World War 2, but concentrated more in recent years on plotting nuclear fallout. Its posts were all disbanded by the end of 1991.

8 Names, ranks and numbers

The technological world is 71% covered by oceans of acronyms and jargon. A brief, two-part guide to these appears below, its second section capturing some of the slang to be heard on the average RAF station. Ranks are hard for the layman to decipher, and so a short course of instruction into their mysteries is herewith appended. Finally, numbers, in the form of an explanation of aircraft accident or repair categories and servicing procedures.

ABBREVIATIONS AND ACRONYMS

A&AEE	Aeroplane & Armament Experimental Establishment
AAM	Air-to-Air Missile
AAR	Air-to-Air refuelling
ACCGS	Air Cadets' Central Gliding School
ADIZ	Air Defence Identification Zone
AEF	Air Experience Flight
AOC(-in-C)	Air Officer Commanding (-in-Chief)
ATC (1)	Air Traffic Control
ATC (2)	Air Training Corps
ATF	Andover Training Flight
Attack	Offensive action with conventional weapons (cf Strike)
BBMF	Battle of Britain Memorial Flight
CATCS	Central Air Traffic Control School
CFS	Central Flying School
COC	Combat Operations Centre
CRC	Control and Reporting Centre
CRP	Control and Reporting Post
CTF	Canberra Training Flight
DRA(AD)	Defence Research Agency (Aerospace Division)
ECM	Electronic Countermeasures
EFTS	Elementary Flying Training School
ELINT	Electronic Intelligence (gathering)
EOD	Explosive Ordnance Disposal
ESM	Electronic Support Measures
ETPS	Empire Test Pilots' School
F3OEU	Tornado F3 Operational Evaluation Unit
FTS	Flying Training School
HAS	Hardened Aircraft Shelter
IAM	Institute of Aviation Medicine

IUKADGE	Improved UKADGE
MRR	Maritime Radar Reconnaissance
MoD(PE)	Ministry of Defence (Procurement Executive)
OCU	Operational Conversion Unit
Pave Spike	Laser designation pod
Paveway	Laser guided bomb
PRU	Photographic Reconnaissance Unit
QRA(I)	Quick Reaction Alert (Interceptor)
RAuxAF	Royal Auxiliary Air Force
RIC	Reconnaissance Interpretation Centre
RP	Reporting Post
RRS	Regional Reinforcement Squadron
SAOEU	Strike/Attack Operational Evaluation Unit
SATCO	Senior Air Traffic Control Officer
SARTU	Search And Rescue Training Unit
SKTF	Sea King Training Flight
SOC (1)	Sector Operations Centre
SOC (2)	Struck Off Charge
Strike	Offensive action with nuclear weapons (cf Attack)
SSR (1)	Secondary Surveillance Radar
SSR (2)	SACEUR's Strategic Reserve
TQF	The Queen's Flight
TTTE	Trinational Tornado Training Establishment
TWCU	Tornado Weapons Conversion Unit
UKADR	United Kingdom Air Defence Region
UKADGE	United Kingdom Air Defence Ground Environment
UAS	University Air Squadron
VASS	Visiting Aircraft Servicing Squadron
VDF	Vulcan Display Flight
VGS	Volunteer Gliding School

RAF-SPEAK

Bimble	Meander, wander (replaces 'stooge')
Bimble Box	Packed lunch
Bluey	Airmail letter form
Bone Dome	Flying helmet
Boss	Squadron commander
Bunny Suit	Aircrew's thermal underclothing
Chippie	De Havilland Chipmunk T10

Christmas Tree	Aircraft robbed of parts to service others
F3	Panavia Tornado F3
F-4 Minus 1	Panavia Tornado F3 (in Phantom-speak)
Fat Albert	Lockheed C-130K Hercules C1/C3
Gozome	Anything concerning the end of an overseas tour
GR1	Panavia Tornado GR1
GR3/GR5/GR7	BAe Harrier GR3/GR5/GR5
Green Writing	Information on a computer display screen or HUD
Groupie	Group Captain
Hangar Queen	Notoriously and regularly unserviceable aircraft
Hindenburgers	Tornado F3's 495 gallon drop-tanks
JP	BAC Jet Provost T3A/T5/T5A
Kit	Almost any piece of equipment or apparatus
Low-Viz	Low visibility paint scheme for aircraft
Meccano	Shorts S312 Tucano T1
MoD Plod	Ministry of Defence Policeman
Noddy Suit	NBC protection clothing
Prod	Engagement of an in-flight refuelling drogue
Rag	Runway arrestor gear
Shadow Squadron	
	Reserve Squadron wartime identity of an OCU
Stash	Station Commander (pronounced 'stay-shh')
Talking Freight	Navigator (in pilot-speak)
Tits-up	Unserviceable
Up To Speed	Functioning correctly
Whistling Handbag	
	Hand-held electric ventilator for AR5 respirator
Winder	AIM9 Sidewinder AAM
Wokka	Boeing Helicopters Chinook HC1B (absorbed from Army-speak)
Zap	Unauthorised unit badge application on a visiting aircraft

RANKS

Two separate career streams are open to those joining the RAF: non-commissioned or commissioned.

Non-commissioned

Rank	Arm badge
● Aircraftman	nil
● Leading Aircraftman	Two-bladed propeller
● Senior Aircraftman	Three-bladed propeller
● Junior Technician	Four-bladed propeller
● Corporal	Two chevrons
● Sergeant	Three chevrons
● Chief Technician	Three chevrons and four-bladed propeller
● Flight Sergeant	Three chevrons and crown
● Warrant Officer	The Royal Arms

Note: Sergeant, Flight Sergeant and Warrant Officer *aircrew* add the RAF eagle above their chevrons or below the Royal Arms. (The debate surfaces within the RAF every few years of whether its badge depicts an eagle or an albatross. The insignia, authorised on 15 September 1949 is officially described: 'In front of a circle inscribed with the motto "Per Ardua Ad Astra" and ensigned with the Imperial Crown, an eagle volant and affrontee, head lowered and to the sinister'.)

Commisioned

Rank	Insignia
● Pilot Officer	Thin band
● Flying Officer	Medium band
● Flight Lieutenant	Two medium bands
● Squadron Leader	Medium, thin, medium bands
● Wing Commander	Three medium bands
● Group Captain	Four medium bands
● Air Commodore	One thick band
● Air Vice Marshal	One thick, one medium bands
● Air Marshal	One thick, two medium bands
● Air Chief Marshal	One thick, three medium bands
● Marshal of the RAF	One thick, four medium bands

Note: All bands are dark blue with a light blue centre. Thin $\frac{1}{4}$ inch; medium $\frac{9}{16}$ inch; thick $1\frac{3}{4}$ inch.

Cadet and probationary ranks are not included, although university students will fly BAe Bulldogs in the rank of Acting Pilot Officer. WRAF ranks are comparable.

Qualification badges

Within certain limits, trade and qualification badges are worn irrespective of rank. Ground trades such as telecommunications, PT Instructor and musician have their own badge, as do voluntary qualifications including marksman and member of a mountain rescue team. Air Steward and Flight Nursing Attendant have two-winged *arm* badges. Aircrew qualifications are worn on the left chest in the form of a pair of wings for pilots and a single wing for other airborne qualifications. The single-wing design includes an appropriate letter or symbol, those in current use being: 'AE' (Air Electronics); AT (Airborne Technician); E (Engineer); FC (Fighter Controller); LM (Air Loadmaster); N (Navigator); S (Air Signaller); and, parachute symbol (Parachute Jumping Instructor). These badges may be worn when the qualification has expired through lack of practice and in extremely rare cases individuals can wear two half-wings following a change of career. Medal ribbons (if any) are worn below the wings and can include campaign awards (Cyprus, South Atlantic 1982, etc) and civil honours (OBE, MBE, etc) as well as decorations for airborne service and gallantry.

INCIDENT AND ACCIDENT CATEGORIES

Since 1952, the RAF has used a numbering system for classifying aircraft unserviceability states and indicating, approximately, the degree of effort required to return them to to the air. It is popularly supposed that when an aircraft is issued with a Category number that it has been involved in an accident; in fact, aircraft are also thus classified when out of service for overhaul or modification.

Classifications and their meanings are:
● **Category 1**   Undamaged or unaffected.

● **Category 2**   Rectification possible with resources of the operating unit.

● **Category 3**   Requires attention of specialist RAF unit, as beyond the resources of operating unit.

● **Category 4**   Can not be repaired on site; requires transportation to the manufacturer's premises

● **Category 5**   Struck off charge as:
Cat 5C   reduced to components
Cat 5FA   flying accident
Cat 5GA   ground accident
Cat 5GI   ground instruction airframe
Cat 5M   missing
Cat 5S   scrap

SERVICING INTERVALS

Most aircraft servicing is based on hours flown, rather as that for a car is determined by mileage. The majority of this work can be accomplished at station level, either by the squadron or the base engineering wing, but 'Majors' are normally undertaken at St Athan or by the contractor. The interval between 'Majors' determines the frequency of other work, and on entry of an aircraft into service is set at an arbitrary level. As experience builds, that can be extended, a case in point being the Tornado GR1 which began with 1,200hr and has been raised to 1,600hr and now 2,000hr. In these cases the servicing intervals were and are as below:

Servicing	Hours between servicings		
● Primary	75	100	125
● Primary Star	150	200	250
● Primary	225	300	375
● Minor	300	400	500
● Primary	375	500	625
● Primary Star	450	600	750
● Primary	525	700	875
● Minor Star	600	800	1,000
● Primary	675	900	1,125
● Primary Star	750	1,000	1,250
● Primary	825	1,100	1,375
● Minor	900	1,200	1,500
● Primary	975	1,300	1,625
● Primary Star	1,050	1,400	1,750
● Primary	1,125	1,500	1,875
● Major	1,200	1,600	2,000

Servicing intervals are different in the case of civil airliners such as the RAF's TriStars. These are overhauled on a calendar basis with an hours 'back-stop' which is only reached with — what is for military operations, but not civil — unusually high utilisation. TriStar data is: Primary, three months or 450hr; Primary Star, six months/950hr; Primary Two Star 12 months/1,800hr; Minor, 24 months/3,600hr; and major, 48 months/7,200hr. For a combat aircraft, 7,200hr would represent a respectable lifetime of 20 years. Existing Canberras have flown 6,000-9,000hr since the early-1950s, the record perhaps being held by WH670 which retired in November 1990 with 10,003. Even Jet Provost T3A XM461 accumulated 8,075hr of 'circuit-bashing' between May 1960 and 6 June 1991, when it was retired. Very few of the last Lightnings in service had passed 4,000hr, but when the RAF bought its second-hand VC10s, for

K2/K3 tanker conversion, they each had some 45,000hr 'on the clock'.

FATIGUE INDEX

Following its Major overhaul, the aircraft returns to the beginning of the cycle, which may be repeated several times during its lifetime. With regular replacement of parts, an aircraft *can* be made to last for ever, but in practice it begins its flying career with a life reckoned in fatigue points. The expected life is termed '100 Fatigue Index' and after each sortie engineers keep tally of the stresses to which a machine has been subjected — helped by on-board counting equipment in the most modern aircraft. Some machines will be withdrawn before reaching 100 and some after; the 100 points is purely an arbitrary number beyond which it is expected that maintenance of the aircraft will become disproportionately costly. Interestingly, because they were required for important work, aircraft in the Victor K2 fleet had their expected lives extended by 27% to 127FI and some have been further inspected and modified to fly to 132FI. Hours on individual airframes with the same FI vary, as those former Victor B2(SR)s which cruised on high-altitude reconnaissance sorties suffered less fatigue than B2s practicing low-level penetration.

Category 5S. Phantom FGR2 XV464 'AN' of No 92 Squadron (the 3,255th F-4 built) arrived at No 23 MU, Aldergrove (now disbanded) on 25 April 1969. It served with No 14 Squadron in the strike/attack role and with No II Squadron for reconnaissance before becoming an air defence aircraft with Nos 19, 56 and 92 Squadrons, plus No 228 OCU. Its last flight was into Wattisham on 12 July 1991 and after removal of engines and useful parts it was placed on the dump to await the arrival of the scrap-merchant during 1992. *Paul Jackson*

Addenda

As identified in the Introduction, the RAF is undergoing a significant reorganisation, the better to operate within the new strategic situation of the 1990s.

During the production of this book there have been a number of changes to be noted. The page reference indicates the first (but not necessarily the only) mentions of the fact:

p9 — *Benson* – On 1 June 1992 No 60 Squadron formed with Wessex HC2s.

p12 — *Finningley* – METS became No 45 (Reserve) Squadron on 1 July 1992.

p13 — *Harrington* – will be retained as HQ of the RAF regiment. Rapier SAMs of No 66 Squadron (ex West Raynham) from 1994.

p15 — *Mount Pleasant* No 1435 flight has now equipped with the Tornado F3.

p16 — *St Mawgan* – No 42 Squadron disbands 1 October 1992 and immediately becomes the 'shadow' of No 236 OCU at Kinloss.

p17 — *Wyton* – No 1PRM was reformed on 1 July 1992 with No 39 (Reserve) Squadron. See also pp26, 31.

p19 — *Aldergrove* – Now has Nos 72/ 230 Squadrons (Wessex/Puma).
Farnborough – The Institute of Aviation Medicine no longer runs a Jaguar T2A.

p21 — *RAF Germany* – will become No 2 Group, Strike Command, on 1 April 1993. The transport and tanker force of No 1 Group will become No 38 Group on 1 November 1992.

pp24, 64 — *No 18 Squadron* – Added Puma HC1s on 30 April 1992. Will transfer to Laarbruch in March 1993.

p25 — *No 27 Squadron* – disbands on 1 October 1992 to become the 'Shadow' of the No 240 OCU at Odiham.

p26 — *No 38 (Reserve) Squadron* – disbanded 1 October 1992 (replaced by No 42 (Reserve) Squadron).
No 39 (Reserve) Squadron – Based at Wyton under Strike/18 Group with Canberra PR9s. Formed from 1 PRU on 1 July 1992.
No 55 Squadron – to become the 'shadow' of No 241 OCU on 1 January 1994.
No 56 Squadron – Disbanded June 1992 now a reserve squadron, F3 OCU.
No 57 Squadron – became the 'Shadow' of No 242 OCU on 1 July 1992.
No 65 (Reserve) Squadron – Disbanded 1 July 1992.

p27 — *No 74 Squadron* – replaces No 3 Training Squadron at No 4FTS, Valley, on 1 October 1992.
No 79 Squadron – will not be re-formed in 1992.
No 92 (Reserve) Squadron reformed at Clivenor on 1 September 1992, replacing No 151.
No 120 Squadron – Some aircraft carry 'CXX' markings.
No 151 (Reserve) Squadron – disbanded 30 August 1992.
No 201 Squadron – some aircraft carry a seagull badge.

p29 — *No 206 Squadron* – some aircraft carry an octopus badge.
No 208 Squadron – will disband on 1 April 1994 and become a reserve Squadron at No 4FTS (replacing No 2 Training Squadron).
No 230 Squadron stood down in Germany on 30 April 1992 and was re-established at Aldergrove on 4 May 1992.

p30 — *No 229 OCU* – On 1 July 1992 redesignated *F30CU*, No 56 (Reserve) Squadron. Badge a phoenix.
No 242 OCU became *Hercules OCU*, No 57 (Reserve) Squadron on 1 July 1992.

p31 — *No 1 PRM* See *No 39 (Reserve) Squadron*.

p32 — *RAFSC* becomes Logistics Command in 1993.